WHY BE CATHOLIC?

+

William J. O'Malley, S.J.

CROSSROAD • NEW YORK

This Printing 2005

The Crossroad Publishing Company
16 Penn Plaza, 481 Eighth Avenue, New York, NY 10001

Printed in the United States of America

Library of Congress Cataloging-in-Publication Data

O'Malley, William J.
    Why be Catholic? / William J. O'Malley
       p. cm.
    ISBN 0-8245-1428-9; 0-8245-1362-2 (pbk.)
    1. Catholic Church—Apologetic works. 2. Religions. I. Title
BX1752.045 1993   93-17605
                                              CIP

*This book is
for
The Kennedys
Susan   Dan   Mimi   Jim
Nancy   Gerry
and
Steve*

This is the big fact about Christian ethics: the discovery of the new balance. Paganism had been like a pillar of marble, upright because proportioned with symmetry. Christianity was like a huge and ragged and romantic rock, which, though it sways on its pedestal at the slightest touch, yet, because its exaggerated excrescences exactly balance each other, is enthroned for a thousand years. . . . It is only a matter of an inch, but an inch is everything when you are balancing.

— G. K. Chesterton, *Orthodoxy*

Contents

Introduction

A Presumption and an Assumption

THIS BOOK PRESUMES NOTHING — except "some kind" of belief in "some kind" of God. Or (to ask even less) it presumes a reader at least slightly uncomfortable saying, "There is no God." The focal question, then, is: If there is "some kind of God," what connection does that belief have to do with practicing some kind of formal, organized religion? Then further, why should that religion be Christian? Or Catholic?

When I use the word "God," I don't mean (at first) even to restrict the content to God as viewed by any particular religion. Not specifically Yahweh — or Jesus — or Allah or Manitou. I merely mean that this book presumes the reader accepts *some* kind of Mind Behind It All, which — at least at the outset — is the sole content of the word "God": a Being responsible for the universe, who had a purpose in creating it all — and a purpose in inviting me to exist. Just as a clockmaker expects his work to keep accurate time (or else it's a bad clock), God expected planets would submit to the laws of attraction and repulsion, crocuses would pop up in spring and not July, lions would forage for food and mate in the proper season and take care of their young.

That's where the problems arise. At the tail end of that evolutionary progress of planet-to-crocus-to-lion came human beings. Up to that point, everything had gone relatively smoothly: planets obeyed the plan programmed into their natures, crocuses obeyed, lions obeyed. Then suddenly along came human beings, the only entities in the whole Cosmic Dance that *don't* have to obey their programming — which makes us vastly different from merely more complex developments of the matter and vegetable and animal stuff that was there before we arrived on the scene.

No planet or crocus or lion can violate its nature. No planet gets fed up with whirling and puts on the brakes; no crocus refuses to take in nourishment; no lion can reject the hassle of dealing with its mate and become celibate. Only human beings can reject their programming — refuse to be human and act instead like clods, or vegetables, or beasts.

1

That undeniable fact is what Western thinkers have called "original sin," which may or may not be traceable back to a naked couple named Adam and Eve, but is nonetheless a fact: Human beings mess up. Human reluctance to obey its own nature is the only Christian doctrine you can prove conclusively from the daily newspapers.

What's more, only human beings can *transcend* their programming, go *beyond* their apparent limitations. On the physical level, only human beings — of all the entities we know of — are not prisoners of their programming. If a new Ice Age hunches its shoulders over the horizon, we don't go around mooing helplessly, waiting for death; we bump off a caribou and put on its skin; we invent fire. If our programming hasn't provided us with wings, we have the wits to make them for ourselves.

On the mental level, we're without any equal (we know of) in the whole universe. Oh, we share brains with all the animals; the core of the human brain is the same as any snake's (from which most of our problems arise); we're special, even though we're still incompletely evolved. Unlike the smartest of beasts (porpoises, for instance), human beings can anticipate the not-even-dreamed-of; we can calculate, measure, ponder, philosophize. The smartest animal is not about to send a spaceship to Mars, or balance a budget, or write *King Lear,* or run a rock concert to feed hungry strangers. No animal ravages its soul to comprehend why those it loves must die. Animals can *know,* but only human beings can — to some degree — *understand.*

The key difference between humans and animals is conscience. As far as we know, no tiger goes into a village, gobbles a lamb, and lurches back into the forest mumbling, "Oh, *God!* I did it *again!* I've got to get counselling!" Animals don't; humans do. At least *good* humans do.

What's more, that fusion of the peculiarly *human* mind and body generates a third entity: a self — what philosophers have always called (for want of a better name) the "soul." It is the self-conscious "I," which is the sum of all my experiences, a unique *person* who never existed before and never will be reduplicated. It is that self, that soul — which is neither body nor mind — that many philosophers believe is imperishable. It is an entity generated and temporarily rooted in time and space but not permanently dependent on time and space. Unlike planets and crocuses and lions, the human self will survive death. Despite our similarities to material beings, to vegetable beings, to animal beings, human beings possess in themselves something — the soul — that is not material. It is our special and unique "fellowship" with the Mind Behind It All, the God who — because he created it all — exists *outside* it all. And so, too, our souls exist at this very moment outside it all.

So. This book presumes only that the reader has at least some vague belief in a God, and it assumes that the reader has messed up at least once — proving that, if there is a God, God is surely not *us*.

First, there is some kind of Mind Behind It All — and thus everything in the universe was intended and has a purpose programmed into it. Second, the book takes as an unarguable given that human beings often refuse to be humane — but also very often surprise us with extraordinary displays of creativity and selflessness and "beyond-it-all."

Transcendent Inter-Communication

"Transcendent Inter-Communication" is a jawbreaker, but it got your attention. What I mean by the term is simply what simpler souls call "praying." But I gave it a hoked-up title to show that I mean considerably more than simply kneeling in a quiet place and rattling off Our Fathers and Hail Marys. Nor do I mean even the far more public formal prayers involved in liturgies — whether they are Masses or Seder services or rain dances.

What I mean by "praying" is centering the self — going deep into that unique soul that is in some way connected beyond time and space into the Mind Behind It All — and communicating directly to one's Ultimate Source. (Perhaps a crude analogy but, if it helps, think of it as withdrawing for awhile and connecting into the Pool of Energy that is the source of all that exists, to "charge your batteries.")

If my presumption is correct, and there is a God who's the cause of all that exists, including you and me, then several corollaries immediately follow. First, if God caused me, then I quite obviously didn't cause God. Neither did you. God caused us both. Now, I don't mean that God forced your parents to do You-Know-What, or even that God — necessarily — stopped at each embryo and breathed a soul into it, as he does in the story of Adam. (Although, being God, he could have easily done that if he wanted to; triggering the Big Bang was a far larger job.) But God created a universe in which the whole process of evolution could take place — from planets, to crocuses, to lions, to us: intelligent beings a quantum leap above our nearest animal cousins. God is the Inventor of the human soul and thus, ultimately, the Inventor of you and me.

Secondly, if the universe is, indeed, a Great Dance in which each participant has its own unique purpose, then God is the Choreographer or Director — not me. I may not be quite satisfied with the part I've been given — my height, my parents, going to work or school — but it's the part I have. I'm free to improvise with it; it's not a scripted part;

I'm not a puppet; each of us is free *not* to be human. I can even pretend to be the Lead.

I may not like the way the play was going when I first came on — the previous history of the world, the other actors I have to perform with. I may not like the fact that, at the end, my character dies. But it's the only play there is. If I go to the Director and ask, "Why do I have to leave the stage?" God can say, "Who gave you the right to a part in the first place?"

Another bombshell, then. One of the toughest admissions one has to make is that, if there is a God, we are answerable to God; God's not answerable to us — as Job discovered so painfully.

Which brings me back to the first bombshell: God is the ultimate source of my existence. I'm dependent; I'm indebted. Granted, if I hadn't been given existence, I'd never know the difference. But I *do* exist, and I'm grateful for that. And not only for the bare gift of existence, but for everything that came with it: my Mom and Dad, the people I love, and babies, and books, and beer, and the Pacific at sunset, and giraffes, and sex, and "Star Wars" movies, and . . . and. . . .

If you tried just to list all the wonderful, joyous, delicious extras that came along with the initial invitation, it'd take the rest of your life. In fact, there are so many fantastic gifts (most of which we take for granted, as if we'd done something to *deserve* them), that it's enough to take the sting out of the (few, in comparison) lousy things we have to put up with — like death, and visits to the dentist, and Saddam Hussein.

There was an important reason for emphasizing "deserve" in that last paragraph. We do take existence — and all those billions of nifty gifts that came along with it — for granted, as if it were something *due* to us. But it wasn't, because before you were given existence, you weren't. How could something that doesn't exist "deserve" anything?

Your existence was pure gift — from God and (no matter what their inevitable faults) your parents. Hard as it is even to imagine, your parents could have lived blissfully ever after without you. But instead, of their own free will, they decided to have you instead of a swimming pool, even at the price of dirty diapers, croup, teething, sleepless nights, temper tantrums, battles about Mass. It might be nice to thank them for that sometime. But ordinarily we — well — take it for granted.

Same with God. He invented You-Know-What, and evolution, and mountains at sunrise, and fields of buttercups, and the whole great Cosmic Dance. And God invited you to join it! It might be nice to thank God for that sometime. But ordinarily we — well — take it for granted.

You may well be self-reliant, but you are most definitely not self-*sufficient*. "I did it all myself!" Untrue.

Take an analogy. Suppose a zillionaire stopped you at random on the street and said, "Now you look like a very promising person to me." And he takes out a roll of bills the size of a tractor tire and peels off a cool million smackerolas. "There ya go. I'd really like you to spend it wisely, but no strings. Use it as you want. Have a nice day." And off he goes.

Now if you didn't even try to find out who the guy was, if it's too much bother even to try to track him down and say at least, "Uh, thank you," I think I'd be justified in calling you an iron-hearted, mean-spirited, conscienceless S.O.B. And while you're at it, it might not be a bad idea (even for purely selfish reasons) to say, "Ah, excuse me, sir, but you seem to know the score, I mean how things work. Could you maybe give me a little advice? I mean, what do you mean when you say, 'Spend it wisely.' I'm new at this millionaire thing, and I need some help, okay?"

Same with God. If you take the gift of existence and all the wonders that go with it, and you don't even try to find out who the Guy is, if it's too much bother even to try to track Him down and say at least, "Uh, thank you," I think I'd be justified in calling you an iron-hearted, mean-spirited, conscienceless S.O.B. And while you're at it, it might not be a bad idea to say, "Ah, excuse me, Sir, but You seem to know the score, I mean how things work, could You maybe give me a little advice? I mean, what do you mean when You say, 'Spend it wisely.' I'm new at this being human, and I need some help, okay?"

It's not that we don't have the time, or that we forget. Very few of us are so busy or absent-minded that we forget to take a shower or brush our teeth.

Part of the reason we don't pray (unless we're in a jam) is that we've never really thought about how much we owe the Mind Behind It All, God, our Father. But if you've read this far, that is, alas, no longer an excuse.

Part of the reason also is that, even when we do realize our indebtedness, we don't like to be beholden; we tend to avoid our bookies and pawnbrokers and loan-sharks when we owe them; we don't go inviting them for long companionable walks in the woods. But that alibi won't work either. Like the zillionaire, God says, "No strings." As we saw, God made us the only entities in the universe who can say, "Kiss off" to him; God made us with a program — a nature — we don't have to follow if we choose not to.

"Oh, yeah. Well, what about the commandments?" What about them? We've all broken at least a few of them, haven't we? And which of us has been struck by lightning? The commandments — and laws and "all those rules" — are simply the results of wise men and women studying the human programming and trying to spell it out in words. But even if the rules of that programming are hammered out in stone, you're still free to do what you damn well please — even to act like a beast, or a vegetable, or a clod.

In fact, probably the best way to thank God for the gifts of existence is to use God's gifts wisely — to find out what human beings are for and try to do your best at it. Yet good atheists and ethical humanists try to do that: to be as human as they can be. You only have one time around; you might as well do a good job of it. But atheists and ethical humanists don't know they're indebted; they feel no need to say at least "Thanks." Unlike them, you and I do.

The Church

"All right. No more guilt trips. I'll pray. But why can't I just go out into the woods and spend time with God? Why do I have to go to some boring ceremony, with all those phonies who look pious for an hour a week and then spend the rest of the week with their fists in the cashbox? And all those rules!"

There you have just about all the usual objections from those who do honestly believe in God but do not want to involve themselves in an organized Church or weekly common worship.

Whenever I hear them (and I've heard them almost as often as God's heard the Our Father), I say, "No problem! In fact it's highly recommended. Only two questions: first, when's the last time you actually *did* it?" Stops them dead in their tracks nearly every time. "And second, why does it have to be either/or? Why can't it be both?"

And that's where we finally come to the questions of this book: Why belong to an organized religion — with formal rituals and "all those rules"? And, specifically, why belong to the Roman Catholic Church?

My best guess about why I'm a Roman Catholic is, *basically,* exactly the same as why I'm male, white, Irish, Democrat, and American: *basically,* I had nothing to do with any of those things. The male part was sheer chance. The rest of those qualities — like my very existence itself — I owe to my parents, and their parents. Originally, I didn't *choose* to be any of those things, any more than I rationally chose to be toilet-trained. The white and Irish parts even my parents had no say in. But the American part and the Democrat part they both chose, and I just sort of "accepted" those — simply by not rejecting them. At first. The same thing was true about my being Catholic. That was my parents' choice and — for a long time — their choice became my "choice," exactly as my Dad's preference for well-done roast beef became my "choice."

But then I grew up.

A child's superego "tapes" everything his or her parents say, as sternly and permanently as the Ten Commandments. What's more, those "laws" were taped with the same emotional intensity that the child felt when his or her parent issued the command.

Thus: "If I ever catch you going to bed without pajamas, I'll whack your butt!" is taped as strongly and unerasably as, "If you miss Mass, you'll go to hell" (Later, when hell lost its effectiveness, it became "You won't get the car Friday night.")

The process of adolescence is supposed to be the time when a person establishes his or her own Ego, a conscience. It's the time to test out what parents said, for oneself, and find which of the "laws" are true and which are merely parents' personal preferences (like well-done roast beef). Unfortunately (because thinking takes effort), many people either, on the one hand, slavishly adopt their parents' opinions or, on the other hand, reject them totally — even the opinions that are true — simply because they *are* their parents' opinions.

From the beginning of my adolescence until I was about thirty, I was in a process of "conversion": opening horizons, testing out my taped "convictions," discovering the parts of myself that were non-negotiable (Irish, white, male) and the parts that were up for discussion (Democrat, Catholic, dark roast beef). I was, to all intents and purposes (as I suspect you are) a Catholic who had been baptized, *but not yet converted* — like the subjects of a pagan king who converted to Christianity and then forced the subjects to be baptized, too, not as a result of their choice but as a result of his choice. What such a "Christian" had to do was decide whether this really was the way he or she wanted to go. Or whether it was a far better idea, no matter how tedious and time-consuming, to go back to the first wrong turn and start off in the right direction.

This book asks: Is the question of being Roman Catholic the same as the question of how you like your roast beef cooked, or the same as the question of your being of some ethnic group, or the same as the question of your being a Democrat or a Republican or an Independent?

I'd hope that it would be at least as important as any of those questions.

Chapter 1

Unzipping the Cocoons

"**L**EAVE ME ALONE!" Does anybody really mean that, seriously? Oh, for awhile maybe, when you're in a snit, when you'd rather eat parsnips than apologize to a friend, but not too many can play the hermit too long. We're *social* beings; we need relationships. Something so consistent that it must be an essential part of *being* human just won't let us bury ourselves for too long. And the worst punishment — sometimes crueler than death — is solitary confinement.

Each of us is at the center of two sets of circles of relationships, some overlapping and closer to home, and some concentric and widening outward.

Most people in the overlapping circles of relationship closest to the center (YOU) know one another as well as you. And you wandered into those circles more or less by accident or because of other people's choices: your family, your neighborhood, your pals, people at work or school. A few of those tighter relationships, though, you chose — if not with all the care of a doctor's diagnosis, at least with a lot of intuitive certainty of the "rightness" of this relationship: your spouse, your steady, the friend you can tell your most painful secrets.

The concentric circles widening outward are a different matter — the relationships you have with your career and with a larger and larger radius of more adult concern: the neighborhood action committee, the union, the city you live in, the United States, the whole world community, and perhaps even beyond that into the Family of God — which goes beyond time and space and death. That web of relationships is quite different from the first. For one thing, it's not so warm and tightly knit; for another, many of the people in your family and neighborhood don't know the people you deal with in that wider circumference. Just as important is the fact that those much wider concentric circles you usually choose to enter — or not — by your own free decision. Except for wartime, when someone is conscripted into service, no one can really be forced to broaden his or her horizons beyond the tight overlapping and

9

warm relationships immediately at hand and the slightly broader scope of one's career.

Yet most people I've known who served in the armed forces — no matter how appalling their experiences were — say that time was the most fully exhilarating period of their entire lives. Why?

Most people content themselves only with that first interlocked set of circles: family, pals to play golf with or carpool with, a few you feel comfortable with at work or at school. And that's about as wide as the radius of their lives gets. And then they die. But it's been a nice life. More or less.

Another one of those bombshell questions: how big a life do you want to lead?

Most people I've known have really wanted to spend the only life they have "being *somebody*." Not just some temporary "somebody" who manages to make it onto "The Tonight Show" or into the checkout-counter tabloids, but somebody who's made a *difference*. Maybe — almost surely — not the same kind of world-changing differences made by somebodies like Martin Luther King, Jr., or Hitler, or Mother Teresa, or the Ayatollah. Bit too intimidating. They want just to have done some small but important thing that means the world is a bit better for their having been here.

That's so constant I have to suspect that urge, also, is part of human nature: wanting to make a difference. But, like all calls programmed into human nature, you can deny that urge, too, or answer it in a much narrower way than you might have.

Raising, nurturing, and protecting a good family is not a bad contribution at all. Having been a person who's always there when anybody in that tight circle of friends is in need is also not a bad epitaph at all. Doing a job that earned the respect of your employers or teachers is not bad at all. Except that it's so external. And it's smaller than it really has to be. All those judgments on my worth — the Arsenio Show, the Nobel Prize, my family, my friends, my work — are all outside me.

Once a man or woman, young or old, consciously or unconsciously, sets a limit to his or her "expansion," he or she has — more or less — set a limit to what life can yield to him or her. As the late Rosalind Russell said, "Life is a banquet! And most poor bastards are starving to death."

They don't have to. Apparently, they "choose" to.

Once people get out of school into "the real world," how many raise up the hedges and lock the doors and settle for the small, tightly circumscribed world of the warm and overlapping relationships? Nice lives, but quite "small," more's the pity. They really want to be "somebody," but being somebody is just too intimidating; it takes too much time; it's just too big a risk.

How many people do you know who read anything they really don't have to — except maybe *Time* (to kill time) and the newspaper (not out of genuine concern but to be up on the daily gossip)? How many do you know who read novels (without a threat or a deadline) any more challenging than what it takes to kill time while they're getting a tan? How many do you know who are active members of P.T.A., or the community action board, or a political party, or give a couple of hours a week to a service project (by their own free choice)? How many "fools" do you know who write letters to the editor? How many do you know who vote? How many people in your classes ever raise their hands and ask a question or make a comment? If you have a manager who is unfair or a teacher who quite obviously doesn't prepare class, how many complain — not just to one another but to someone who might get changes made, until they've been heard? If a few of them asked you to go with them to complain, would you? Or would you be too afraid the boss or teacher might find out and take vengeance?

Bombshell again: how many people spend their lives treading water and then die?

They all want to "be somebody" — to stand out from the faceless crowd. They just don't want to stick their necks out — which is the only way to stand out from a crowd.

A great part of the reason, I think, is a sense of helplessness. "What good can *I* do? The guy next to me in the voting booth told me he'd voted for every single candidate I'd voted *against*. The only purpose I served in 'the electoral process' was to *negate* his vote!" A small contribution. But not nothing.

But what if all — or even a lot — of those who thought they were "nothings" threw off their shyness and spoke — even in a harsh whisper? Ah, the noise! The men who started the American Revolution were quite prosperous farmers and businessmen, content with their small, warm, overlapping circles of relationships. But something in them — something in that human nature that claims fellowship with that evolutionary Mind Behind It All — just couldn't be silent. Alone, each of them was a thin voice crying in the wilderness, but together they moved a nation of nobodies to cry freedom. Abraham Lincoln was just a lawyer; Susan B. Anthony was just a bookish woman; Rosa Parks was just an ordinary old black lady whose feet hurt and was too bushed to get up and give her seat in the bus to a white lady; the people who cried halt to the Vietnam War were just ordinary students and clergy and ticked-off nobodies too fed up to be silent anymore. And, God, did those nobodies make a difference!

The first point to make is: you can't do it alone.

The second point to make is: you're not alone.

Unless you want to be.

Societies: Congregations and Communities

Sadly, most of us sell ourselves too short. What's more, we sell those around us short as well. Each one of us has been hurt, more than once, which tends to make us "shy" — that is to say: distrustful, guarded, perhaps even . . . cowardly. So we begin to erect invisible defenses, barriers against being hurt like that again. But those very barriers also shut us against reaching out and growing.

Very few become hermits, fleeing any kind of conflict into the sanctuary of physical *isolation*. Far, far more become at least in some sense loners, zipping themselves into invisible cocoons with a few tested friends in a sanctuary of psychological *insulation*. They can be aloof even in a ballpark or subway car or classroom. (Or Sunday Mass.) It is a kind of self-protective loneliness, chosen rather than its opposite: sharing.

All self-imposed isolation and insulation is subconsciously egocentric. "What will they think of me? Everybody's watching me!" The humbling — and liberating — truth is that they're not watching you at all! Most are inside their own cocoons, afraid *you're* watching them! If only you could surrender center stage to Someone Else — Someone who actually is the Center of It All — perhaps you might be freed of some of your defenses, free to come out of your protective cocoon, look around, shake hands with all the other fallible, fearful, human beings.

Then maybe we could start getting something done. Not "when are they gonna . . . ?" but "when are *we* gonna . . . ?" Whether we like one another or not, whether we totally trust one another or not, two heads are better than one; a burden shared is a burden halved; many hands make light work; we can get more — each of us — through self-confident cooperation than through self-protective competition. Those are all cliches, but cliches become cliches because they've so often proven true.

"Society tells us that we should. . . . " Whenever I hear that, I bristle. Who is this "society" to tell me or you what we can and can't do? Where is this society's office? If I wanted to bump off him/her/it, where would I go? Society is *us*, and *we* can have a voice in what "society says" — if we're willing to risk surrendering the warm coziness of the self-protective cocoon.

There are two basic kinds of societies: congregations and communities.

Congregations are groups gathered together for some purely utilitarian purpose: the crowd at an airport, citizens of a big city, a coalition government, a student body. Whether they like one another or not, or even know one another, is not important. Their reasons for being together are based only on a common need, which has to be handled by (even grumbling) cooperation rather than by individualism. The very word "congregation" comes from the Latin word *grex:* a herd of sheep.

Communities are also societies, but with a great qualitative difference. Not only do the members have a common interest in a project, but they also have a common interest in one another. Your membership in that first set of interlocking, tight-knit circles is (most often) communitarian: a family, a team, the yearbook staff, the people at work. There are fewer cocoons in a real community. Whereas people in a congregation are merely "adjacent to," people in a community are "with" one another. There may have been a lot of screaming fans who were "with" me at the basketball game, but my friend went with me. We all shared the game, but my friend and I also shared one another.

There is no more common article in a school paper than — at least once every year — "What's Wrong with Our *Spirit?*" The reason for those articles validates everything I've said so far: some have opened themselves up into a larger circle — the school — and found it exciting, enriching, life-giving, but the majority are still cowering with a small circle of friends back in their protective cocoons. The ones who have found "a larger life" want to share it, pull in more to enjoy it and be enjoyed. Alas, they have their work cut out for them. Over the years, the skins on some of those cocoons have become tougher than Teflon.

Most of us have been in airports when the plane is "temporarily delayed" — maybe an hour. We sit around, poke through a magazine, pace, stare. But some lucky times someone leans over and says, "Somebody oughtta sue this airline," and the two of you start swapping stories, and somebody eavesdrops and joins in. That "congregation" of people surely hasn't turned into a "community," but all the people have become just the slightest bit less lonely. And just the slightest bit less afraid the next time the opportunity to reach out and share arises: in an elevator, at the supermarket, in the cafeteria.

And who knows where this momentary opening of the cocoon could lead? Most go nowhere. Just a pleasant way of sharing rather than locking your nose into the small print on your ticket. But sometimes they really become important.

One time my mother was in a coma in the hospital. I sat there by the bed most of visiting hours, but there was nothing I could do. I was edgy and fed up with reading. So I got up and started walking the corridors. I stopped in one open doorway. Inside was a middle-aged man scowling into a hand mirror and pulling at the hairs on the back of his neck. "Hi," says our hero. "Hi," he smiles back. "Something wrong?" I ask. "It's this hair!" he says. "The hospital barber is off for a week, and it's driving me nuts." So, I say, "I cut hair in the seminary. I'll do it for you."

We found a pocket comb and a nail scissors and got his neck more or less cleaned up. Later I stopped by again and met his wife and two daughters, and by the time Mom was well enough for me to go back to the seminary, we'd become "sort of friends." They invited Mom over for dinner; she invited them; I stopped over to see them when I was home. It so happened that when I was sent to teach in Rochester, Pete's daughter was working as a nurse in a Rochester hospital. She started coming to a Mass I said every Sunday at the school. There she met a young unmarried lay teacher who also came to the Mass. Now they're married and have three children.

And it all started with one dumb "Hi!"

Isn't that the way all friendships start?

All it takes is a bit of confidence — in yourself and in the people around you, that you are a pretty good gift to offer and that they really are pretty nice people to offer a gift to. Nine times out of ten, when you offer yourself to someone like that, the other person will not only accept your gift but gift you in return. You will enlarge and enrich both your lives. Of course, one time out of ten, the other person will tell you, "Bug off!" And so, to avoid that one (chance of) rejection, many people give up those nine gifts. They impoverish themselves, and they impoverish *everyone* around them. Pity.

You can make a difference.

You can be somebody.

If you want.

~ Questions for Discussion ~

1. Look around your job or your class. Where are the interlocking circles? Which individuals and groups are the "isolated" and the "insulated"? No need to embarrass anybody by sharing that aloud. Just get the lay of the land, figure out where the resistances to this group's becoming a community are. Where are the conflicting attitudes? Which people could you most count on to help break down those barriers? Which people would resist risking the vulnerability necessary to having a more open relationship?

List all the things the members have in common. Not just the external things like sex, or skin color, or economic background, but more importantly the inner things: the need to succeed, the expectations of family, confusions about sex, the fear of being hoaxed or embarrassed or rejected. Start with questions like "What scares all of us most? What are the things all of us envy in other people?"

Quite likely, you'll find the things everybody in the room shares are far more numerous than the things that differentiate. We all want to count; we all want to make a difference; we all want to be somebody. And we're all afraid of risk.

Now, what can this group do to erode the barriers? Be concrete. Not "We could all change our aloof attitudes." Whatever concrete ways you choose can't be something that only part of the group can get in on — even if it's most of them. A basketball game won't do it; at least a few have no talent. But there might be a unitive possibility if a class decided that, during gym, each of the athletically talented was going to take one unskilled classmate and show him or her how. Same thing could be done showing untalented kids how to dance — or type, or pass math.

In a parish, could everyone pool talents — bankers, lawyers, construction people, do-it-yourself-ers, housewives, kids — and buy an inner-city house to refurbish for a poor family?

What about a party or a dance limited (this time) just to this group? Where? When? Of course it's going to be embarrassing — at least at first. But isn't it worth it?

We all want bigger lives. When's somebody gonna do something about it? Who, if not you? When, if not now?

2. We hear a lot of talk about the Church as a "community," but the way most people act makes the Church merely a "congregation." At the Greeting of Peace, we all dutifully and with some embarrassment unzip our cocoons, reach out quickly, shake hands and flee back inside. That's not the fault of the text of the Mass ("the same old prayers every week").

It's not the fault of the priest, or the choir, or the hokey hymns. As the wise Pogo said, "We have met the enemy, and he is us."

The problem again (after the problem of total indifference to the problem) is a feeling of helplessness. One parishioner is not likely to make a parish revolution. But a group might have a better chance. Draw up an agenda of *concrete* proposals you, as a group, could bring to the pastor or to the parish council, concrete ways in which the people at any Mass — even before the Mass begins — could begin to be less uptight with one another, so that the Mass could become a genuine "celebration" because the people have become a genuine "community" — rather than being both celebration and community in name only.

You can make a difference. If you want.

Chapter 2

Grasping a Society's Soul

ST. EXUPERY, who wrote *The Little Prince,* said, "The essential is always invisible." In a very true sense, *you* are invisible. No one can see the truly you, only your body. They can't see your self — your soul, your who-I-am. They look at the way you make your body work: how you walk, what you say, how your face "betrays" the inner, real self. Then, after a bit of experience with you — or even on the spur of the moment — they formulate an opinion of you. That's all it is, just an "educated" guess, surely not a completely accurate x-ray of your self.

In fact, there are whole galaxies of self even your spouse, your parents, and your best friends may not be totally aware of. Even if your biographer dogged your steps as relentlessly as Boswell dogged Johnson's, there'd still be more to tell. Even a skilled psychologist, using the most sophisticated tests, has to take hours to come up with a (still tentative) opinion of "what makes you tick." Any husband, even after twenty years of marriage, who says he has his wife "all figured out" is a fool.

That's what education is all about: to find out the true *inner* natures of things — including the inner nature of oneself — and then to try to find words that capture that inner nature, tentatively but at least as accurately as you can at the moment, without self-deceptive dodges, and with a willingness to come back later for another look and perhaps some readjustment.

Symbols and Societies

Just as your You — your inner self — is invisible, so is the soul that unites and energizes a society. Congregations are groups of people focused on an *idea* (getting an education, getting to Pittsburgh, getting rid of the fear of hell for missing Mass). Communities are groups of people focused around an *ideal* (raising good and loving children, easing exploitation, sharing our joy and gratitude that we are the sons and daughters of an Eternal God and that we need not fear death).

Just as each of us has to try — as adequately as possible — to express

17

the inner self in concrete words and gestures and facial expressions, so too a society has to embody, physicalize, concretize its invisible ideas and ideals in symbolic writings, symbolic objects and places, and symbolic actions. All those symbols that attempt to embody a society's inner conviction and purpose are the society's *myth*.

Unfortunately, the word "myth" has two conflicting meanings, as opposite to one another as "falsehood" and "truth."

The most frequent use of the word "myth" — even by TV news commentators — is "without any slightest foundation in fact," as in "Vietnam destroyed the myth that America could never lose a war" or "Eventually the myth of Santa Claus dies." That use of the word "myth" is also associated with superstitions: never put a hat on a bed, walk under a ladder, step on a crack. All the word's connotations have to do with being naive, unscientific, and easily hoaxed. That's the analytical, calculating, left-brain use of the word "myth."

But there's another whole side of the brain, the right lobe, which is intuitive, evaluates things in a context rather than in isolation, sees the inner "rightness" of things when there's no conclusive analytical proof (which friends to trust, believing in God). The left, analytical brain is essential to find the truth, but it takes you only so far. And if you rely *only* on the left lobe to find the truth, not matter how smart you are, you are looking half-wittedly. Sort of "mono-lobe" thinking.

The whole truth about anything — who you truly are, the purpose of human beings, the nature of God — is too big and too complex to be reduced *solely* to mere left-brain "data." Take for example SAT scores. They are the result of a long-tested and refined process of analyzing what kind of student one is. The results are "true," in the sense they're correct, but are they the whole truth? They give a *fairly reliable* assessment of one's ability to read, compute, reason. But they're purely a left-brain assessment of only left-brain achievement. No machine-scored test can measure one's hopes, dreams, and ambitions — which are a very great part of who one is, even as a college candidate. There is no way it can evaluate nervousness, motivation, willingness to work hard.

That's why colleges also rely on interviews and letters of recommendation. A skilled admissions officer can "sense" something in a candidate that doesn't show up in the machine-scored test; a sensitive teacher has a "hunch" that, *despite* the scores, you've got the "stuff." All those words — "sense," "hunch," "stuff" — are vague and non-analytical, but they're important.

The left brain carefully hammers out the truth into definitions; the right brain formulates the truth in *symbols*.

Just like analytical definitions, symbols are inadequate (but still useful) attempts to describe realities we can't see in terms or realities we can see. We use symbols all the time, every day, in place of strict definitions, most often because, at least at the moment, symbols do the job better. Love, patriotism, and choosing are all realities; but you can't see them. So, physical roses symbolize the invisible love, a physical flag gives "body" to the invisible patriotism, and a physical crossroads concretizes the invisible necessity of choosing.

The symbol doesn't *equal* the reality, in the sense that, when the roses wilt, the love is dead. Nor does the symbol perfectly *capture* the reality, any more than drawings of atoms are any better than educated guesses about what atoms actually look like. But then again, neither do our *definitions* equal or capture the things they try to describe — no matter how carefully and expertly the definitions are forged, and no matter how naively we think our definitions are "the last word." Lexicographers have been trying to capture "love" in a definition for centuries, but they still haven't come up with one that does it better than the picture of a muddy kid standing in the doorway holding out a bunch of dandelions and saying, "For you, Mommy."

Symbols don't capture realities any more than definitions do, but they're better than nothing. And often they're better than definitions.

Myth as Symbol

Myth in the second sense — completely opposite to the first meaning of "naive delusion" — is a *story* or a *theory* that acts like a symbol: it tries to physicalize a truth (which is, by its very nature, real but invisible). Like a symbol, a myth is predominantly a product of the right brain, although, if you dig below the surface, it usually has a left-brain and quite true assertion at its heart. For instance, Aesop's fable of the turtle and the rabbit never really occurred. And yet it tells a real truth about human life, and Aesop hands that left-brain truth to you the minute he finishes the right-brain story: "Slow and steady wins the race." That's true.

Folktales tell truths, too. Hansel and Gretel says that, sooner or later, children have to get booted out into the woods and find their own way. That's true. Parables never actually occurred either. Jesus and Plato and other wise folk dreamed them up *in order* to tell a truth we'd most likely resist if it were told literally. The parable of the Good Samaritan answers the hard-nosed left-brain question that provoked it: Who is my neighbor? And the answer is: Anybody you meet in trouble along the side of your road — without exception. That's true.

The second story in the book of Genesis is also a myth, a story that never occurred historically but that still tells a truth. The author of Genesis, who lived about the same time as Aesop, surely didn't expect his audience to believe that at one time snakes actually talked to naked ladies in the park, any more than Aesop's audience believed a turtle and rabbit actually decided one day to have a race. But Genesis does tell a profound truth that nobody could deny: put two human beings in paradise and they're gonna mess up. And it also says quite clearly that we're pretty special creations, but we were never intended to "be equal to God." That's true.

Philosophical theories try to give primarily left-brain answers to precisely those kinds of questions: Why do human beings mess up? What is life for? Why do we have to die? Myths try to answer those questions, too, relying a great deal more on the symbol-making power of the right brain — not only in the writer who creates the symbolic answer, but also in the reader who attempts to decipher it. The difference is not that one way is trustworthy and the other is not; the difference is a matter of emphasis. Just as there is beauty in math and strict discipline in poetry, there is a great deal of imagination in philosophy and a great deal of clear thinking in myth.

Back for a moment to a more interesting subject: You. As we saw at the outset of the chapter, the inner truth of who-you-are is invisible. But you "project" that self in concrete ways that enable others — more or less — to figure out what your self is like. That is your *personality*. But there's also another "self" in there, at least a *potential* self: the kind of person you want to be. In a very real sense, it is your conscience: the principles, and ideals and convictions you are at least trying to live up to. Your "philosophy of life." It is your *character*. Your character is your own personally chosen "myth."

Each of us needs a personal philosophy of life, a character that provides a framework for all we do and a fundamental norm when it comes to making choices. Otherwise, our lives are ODTAA: one-damn-thing-after-another. That personal philosophy gives our lives shape, meaning, direction. Without such a framework, our years are nothing more than this job, then that one; this love affair, then that one; this event, then that one. What's more, a philosophy of life — a personal ethic, character, myth — is essential when you're faced with a complicated decision, like whether the pay raise that requires moving to a new city outweighs the pain of the kids' losing their lifetime friends, or whether having an abortion is better than carrying the child and giving him or her up for adoption. You simply can't go back to the start each time and ask all the basic questions all over again: What's life for? What's really important? Where the hell am I going?

That's the basic question your philosophy of life — your ethic, your character, your myth — tries to answer, at least tentatively: Where the hell am I going? Just as that's true of individuals, so it is true of societies.

Most peoples of the earth — societies — have embodied their common beliefs about where the hell we're going into myths and religions. Most of us, as we also saw in the Introduction, inherit our "personal" philosophies of life — even down to the way we like our roast beef — from our parents. Adolescence is the time to sit down for a few years and painstakingly analyze what elements in your inherited philosophy are valid (consistent with the way human life actually is), and what elements are merely the changeable whims of your parents and/or your society.

The part of your inherited myth that says you shouldn't kill people you'd probably still agree to without much argument. However, the parts of your inherited myth that say you should go to Mass, refrain from pre-marital sex, and never cheat are more difficult to go along with, because society's myth (embodied in the media) seems diametrically *opposite* from the philosophy/ethic/myth you got from your parents and from your religion.

Of course, any fool realizes you can't simply dump your parents' myth totally and swap it for the media's myth totally. That's simply exchanging one mental slavery for another. No, forging a genuine personal myth takes a lot of work. Unfortunately, no matter what "original sin" means, it's infected most of us with a high distaste for work — even when what's at risk is the whole meaning of our lives.

That's what education is fundamentally for: to forge a personally validated philosophy/ethic/myth. All the rest is preliminary: learning the basic skills of learning and getting a job-license that says you're not an illiterate. But the real, lasting purpose of education is to find your ideal, your myth. Ethics has nothing to do with religion; even good atheists need an ethic. You need an ethic simply to be a good human being.

After high school, again unfortunately, in the present multiversity there is no single unifying myth, as in "*uni*versity." At least until recently the compulsion has been to *specialize*, early and intensely, in a particular and quite narrow field of learning. Many could go through college without ever having taken a single philosophy course — and perhaps never having cultivated one complete half of their brains: the right half. Even those who have a heavy concentration of philosophy courses often find they've been given so many varying and even contradictory points of view that they end up with a prestigious piece of diploma — but a mind jumbled and baffled about the meaning of human life.

Thus, most people who have uncritically rejected their inherited myth system simply "go with the flow." Most make a fairly decent living. There are unexpected intrusions in their lives, but most of the time their days and weeks are relatively placid. They have pleasant personalities, but not too much discernible character. They're . . . well . . . "just like everybody else." To be perfectly frank, my bet is that you yourself would like to put this book down right here and settle for that.

However, it is undeniably certain that, sooner or later, each of them — and you — is going to face an unplanned-for, major, and unavoidable crisis: a betrayal in love, the loss of a job, an unwanted pregnancy, the death of a loved one. At such momentous crises, decisions have to be made, and anguish and fear won't let you sit down and reason out a whole philosophy of life from scratch. Ironically, the only time you are free to sketch out your myth is when you are relatively at peace — when you least need a myth to give suffering meaning.

That is the one place that every philosopher and mythmaker in history, from Buddha to Karl Marx, always started: suffering. Why do bad things happen to good people? It is one of the major factors that differentiate our species (by a quantum leap) from lower species: *only we know that things aren't what they should be.* No rock, radish, or reptile knows that. But it's the truth, and you don't need a college education to know it's the truth. Kids in ghettoes and migrant camps all know that truth: things aren't what they should be.

So, the first question is: Why do we suffer? And the next question is how *should* things be? And once that's answered: What can we (and can't we) do to make things at least a bit more like what they should be? When you begin to find tentative answers to those three dandy questions, then you begin to forge your own personal philosophy of life.

Pre-Fab Philosophies and Myths

Most of us buy our philosophies and myths "off the rack." We can't afford the time (we think) to tailor-make our own. But someone hardy enough to try to grasp his or her soul and myth, someone who wants to be a person of character, needn't start from absolute scratch. Not to overwork the metaphor, you can shop around among the many basic myths and see if there aren't one or two that "more or less feel right" and need only a few alterations. Or you may spot aspects that ring true even in a myth you don't particularly like overall, but that you'd like to see included in your own. For instance, as a Christian — and even as a Catholic priest — I never understood what praying really meant until I studied Zen Buddhism. There are a lot of things about Buddhism I don't like, particularly its negative response to the physical world, but Buddhist ideas about praying have certainly enriched my own philosophy of life.

There are uncountable answers to those three questions, so we can consider only a few here, and rather sketchily at that. But they will serve at least to give a preliminary overview of how myths serve to embody a society's ideas and ideals.

	Why We Suffer	*What Should Be*	*The Solution*
PRIMITIVES	The fussy gods are angry.	Peace and plenty.	Sacrifice a virgin.
BUDDHISTS	Desire: spirit imprisoned in vicious matter.	Nirvana: Freedom from matter; elimination of self.	Meditation and penance to control body and soul.
MARXISTS	Private property and greed.	Universal equality.	Common ownership of all.
CAPITALISTS	Inertia and laziness.	Material prosperity.	Hard work and competition.
ROCKERS*	Uptightness imprisoning natural Id.	Unlimited freedom.	Rebel, and do whatever comes naturally.

*I include the myth of the rock'n'roll culture not as some kind of joke, but because I believe it does embody a belief about human life, perhaps the most persuasive and pervasive philosophy in the world today. It is everywhere you turn, and the principles that underlie its statements regarding what life is about are accepted as uncritically as any primitive religion.

From each of those clusters of basic insights into human suffering, the myth system develops over time into a whole complex structure of concrete means to bring the myth's answers into everyday life. Each system of values is concretized into *symbolic writings* (stories of the gods and heroes, *The Vedas, The Communist Manifesto, The Wall Street Journal,* "I Can't Get No Satisfaction"), *symbolic objects and places* (totem poles, shrines to the Buddha, hammer and sickle, a paycheck, a punk hairdo), and *symbolic activities* (puberty rites, meditation, May Day parades, scanning the ticker tape, singing along at a concert). Each of those symbols becomes somehow "sacred" within that myth system. The flag, for instance, is nothing more than a piece of cloth, but it is far more than that when someone burns it.

As each system elaborates, it lets us know who the "saints" are (tribal heroes, gurus, cosmonauts, giants of industry, chart-toppers) and also who the "sinners" are (tribes with "false" gods, sensualists, capitalists, communists, conformists). As you can see, those who are saints in one myth are sinners in another.

What's more important for the ordinary member is that he or she gets a sense of *belonging,* in a web of relationships in which he or she takes on a greater meaning than an isolated or insulated individual. One's personal values are bolstered — and challenged — by others who share them. There is a common enterprise in which each of us has a meaningful part, no matter how small it is. That's what a myth system does: it validates one's purpose. The myth system is a measure against which to evaluate your life. Either you submit to someone else's myth and let them tell you what you're worth, or you choose a myth yourself and tailor it to what you honestly believe constitutes a good person: a "saint."

All the philosophies on that graph give genuine insight into human life. Perhaps we're too sophisticated to see much merit in the lifeview of the *Primitive,* the unschooled pagan, and yet there is still a lingering fear in all of us that, when someone we love falls ill, it might be punishment for a sin *we* committed. And the primitives have some pretty nifty rituals — not all that different from a rock concert. What's more, primitives have a more refined "sense" of the "holy and sacred" in storms, desert sunsets, stars over the ocean. They do have something to tell us. And yet, as an overall lifeview, paganism seems a great deal too simplistic, too exclusively right-brain, at least to anyone who has studied physics.

It is true, as *Buddhists* claim, that a great deal of our suffering comes from desiring things that just aren't possible: if only I had different parents, if only I were taller, if only I hadn't done that. But reality challenges the full thrust of the Buddhist lifeview as an overall myth. Life isn't all suffering; there are some very beautiful and enjoyable things in the world to gladden the heart — including many of the very real values dear to the primitives and to the rockers. What's more, the final aim of Buddhism is the total elimination of the self. It is, in a very real sense, a kind of prolonged suicide.

It is true, as *Marxists* claim, that selfishness is at the root of a great many of our problems. Yet there's also something undeniable in our nature that demands at least some things one can call his or her own private property. Nor does that desire seem merely programmed into us by a particular society; no one has to teach a little girl (no matter what her society) that her doll is not common property to be taken away at some other little girl's whim. It is also true that, as an overall philosophy of life, communism just can't work. We are not all equally talented or shrewd or lucky. The game of Monopoly starts out as a perfect communism, everybody equal, but after only a few rounds, there's an imbalance. And after fifty years of trying, Marxism made countless millions miserable. Marxists have something to tell us all, but as an overall myth, their answers have too many loopholes.

It is true, as *Capitalists* claim, that inertia plays a large part in our unhappiness. A man or woman's work gives shape and direction to every week and year of our lives; look at someone recently retired to see how aimless one feels without a job to give getting up in the morning some purpose. Yet, to give rockers their due, work can't be everything. As a character in *Death of a Salesman* says, "Working fifty weeks a year for a lousy summer vacation!" There's got to be more to life than that.

It is true, as *Rockers* claim, that many of us find our lives bogged down in a rat race, that there are very real powers within us strangled by button-down collars and three-piece suits and the straitjacket of other people's expectations. But the truths capitalists cling to are still true: if you're going to live, you have to eat; if you're going to eat, you have to work; if you're going to work, you have to compromise. And the profound weakness in the rocker view of life's purpose is manifested inescapably in the lives of its "saints": Jim Morrison, Janis Joplin, John Belushi, Jimi Hendrix, and so many others. Why would people who have "found the answer" need to anesthetize themselves with drugs? Why would someone who knows the real purpose of life commit suicide?

It is possible to pick up bits and pieces from this myth and that and live them out in your life, even though they logically contradict one another. It is clear, for example, that you can be both a capitalist and a rocker. You can slave away at the 9-to-5 treadmill weekdays and whoop it up drinking and dancing all weekend. And the inconsistency isn't just logical; it's also psychological. Something in the way we're made rebels against living out two antagonistic lifeviews. As so many rock lyrics themselves prove, the so-called "unlimited" weekend freedom makes the workweek unbearable drudgery: "Take this job and shove it!" And the work days are five-sevenths of your life.

The ultimate test of any myth is reality: the way things really are. Any myth that fails the reality test is a false myth. The truth of the myth's validity is not that its devotees are happy all the time. The test is whether they face life — especially suffering — with confidence and peace of mind.

There is one sentence that, I think, captures all that this chapter has been trying to say: Either you submit to someone else's myth and let them tell you what you're worth, or you choose a myth yourself and tailor it to what you honestly believe constitutes a good person: a "saint." Which will it be for you?

~ Questions for Discussion ~

1. Your job or school is a whole myth system, too. How do its most basic convictions about "what people are for" differ from other careers' or schools'? How is that reflected symbolically in its every-day policies? At work: job descriptions, management-worker relations, grievance procedures, relations with customers? At school: curriculum, dress code, discipline, service projects, extracurriculars, athletics, social events? Where in the school is the chapel located? Why? What is the school's focal symbol: Knight, Lion, Bulldog? Why? What's that symbol trying to embody about the school's spirit? Does an athletic letter sweater mean as much today as it did in your mother's and father's day? Why? Budgets are also more revealing symbols of a school's authentic purpose than the school catalogue is. Is the retreat budget as large as the athletic budget? Why?

Remember: the actual day-to-day working-out of a myth doesn't have to be perfect. In fact, it never can be, as we'll see in the next chapter. There's always room for improvement. On a scale of one to ten, how would you rate your work's or your school's actual achievement of the goals it has set itself in the philosophy and objectives (myth) of its brochures or catalogue? If there are loopholes, what could you and a group of like-minded friends actually do, concretely, to change that?

2. As a preliminary test of "all that religious education brainwashing" how does the Catholic Church answer those three basic questions: Why do human beings suffer? How should things be? What are the means by which we can ease human suffering and make things more as they should be?

How does the Church embody the answers to those questions in concrete symbols: symbolic writings, symbolic objects and places, symbolic activities?

Are those symbols — scripture, religious medals, Mass, etc. — as meaningful today as when you were in school or in your mother's and father's day? Why? Are there any of the Church's symbols you do find genuinely effective, meaningful, moving?

Chapter 3

Lowering Your Expectations

THE PURPOSE OF THIS CHAPTER is to lower your expectations of what any myth can deliver — including the Church's myth. By now, it's clear every society and every individual needs a myth — a freely chosen self-ideal — which gives meaning to every element in the society's and the individual's lives (especially to suffering and setbacks), a myth that is a flexible set of guidelines for coping with difficult, unexpected decisions and that gives a purpose to living, a goal to "live up to." But we fall into the fallacy of wanting our myths perfect — both in their theoretical formulation and in their practical execution. No loopholes in the explanations of the myth, no faltering in carrying out the myth in everyday life, so everything is just peachy.

If that's your expectation, you landed in the wrong galaxy. Nothing ever dreamed up and carried out by a human being or a group of human beings is or ever was or ever will be perfect; if it were, it would be God. If Einstein knew what physicists have discovered since he died, he'd be busting to get back and rework his theories; if Beethoven were still around, he'd take the "Eroica" and give it a finer tuning; and if Jesus returned for an inspection tour of the Church today, I have no slightest doubt he'd have a few suggestions. No human theory or practice is incapable of improvement — which *ipso facto* says it's not perfect. If you're expecting your job, school, country, or Church — or yourself — to be flawless, you're shopping for a product that can't be bought. Not anywhere. If you want perfection, you're automatically asking for God. God is the only one who can deliver.

That's one of the "interesting" things about being human: There'll always be something to gripe about.

Now I've never taught anyone — in high school, or college, or graduate school — whose parents or teachers demanded (at least in so many words) that he or she be perfect. Nonetheless, in thirty years I've never taught a single boy or girl, man or woman, who wasn't subconsciously convinced he or she had to be perfect — or else they wouldn't be loved,

27

not just by God, but by their own parents and friends. Where did they get that idea?

Unfortunately, we hear descriptions at assemblies, political conventions, church services, religion classes, that are too often full of exaggerated claims about the way we're living out our myths: "We're Number One!" and "America is all heart!" and "Let us all thank God for the profound love we share here this morning at Mass!" And we end up expecting school and country and Church to live up to those bombastic claims. (The truly *worst* enemies of a cause are its most fanatic adherents!) And we look around and find those claims are just not true: we lost the last three games; 30 million Americans live in poverty; the "loving" people around me in church — and I myself — don't feel too terrific even about shaking hands! The facts prove the claims false.

True, people who make speeches about our shared myths ought to be more careful with their rhetoric. But the blame for our consistent disappointment in our institutions (the concrete expressions of our myths) can be laid as well to the gullible audience. Expecting a myth — either in theory or in practice — to be perfect is as unfair as expecting your doctor to be as ideal as Alan Alda, your father to be as unflappable as Bill Cosby, and your lawyer as keen-minded as Raymond Burr. (You do, don't you?)

The last chapter said that a myth — a societal or personal value system — does not, on the one hand, *equal* the reality it tries to embody, nor does it, on the other hand, *capture* the truths about life about which its members are so convinced. Maybe the best analogy I can find for the inadequate-but-not-negligible value of myths is the maps that early explorers drew long before Columbus. When you contrast them to the maps we have today in an ordinary Woolworth's, or even more when you contrast them with actual photographs of earth from satellites, those old ham-handed parchment maps look ludicrous — compared to the reality. But without those clumsy approximations, Columbus would never have been able to push them further; without Galileo's now primitive sketches of the universe, we'd never be able to send out rockets to the stars.

The same can be said about any pre-fab myth you pick "off the rack" or about your own gradually evolving personal myth: They're never "etched in stone"; they ought always to be evolving, growing, enriching themselves with new insights from other myths that see life from an exciting new angle, one we had never thought of exploring.

Deifying and Demythologizing a Myth

Myths are, after all, trying to take a truth, which is of its nature immaterial, and turn it into something that it is definitely not: material. The two foolish extremes in dealing with myth, are (1) deifying the myth, making it into an idol, acting as if it actually were the perfect answer to all problems, with nothing left to learn or rethink ("My country — or Church, or family, or opinion — right or wrong!"), and (2) demythologizing the myth, damning it entirely for its loopholes, left-braining it down to the bare bones of imperfect men and women trying to pretend they are accomplishing something naively noble ("All those people at Mass on Sunday are hypocrites").

Archbishop Marcel Lefebvre, who broke from the Roman Church for what he thought were excessive compromises in Vatican II, is an example of the first inflexible attitude: deifying the myth; Carl Sagan, who reduces belief in intangible realities to superstitious gibberish, is a pretty good example of the second inflexible attitude: demythologizing the myth.

The first extreme takes the myth as if it were literally true and perfect; the opposite extreme takes the myth as if it were utterly false and useless. Neither extreme, of course, is true — or fair. The truth — reality — lies between the two. On the one hand, we need commonly held convictions and symbols that remind us of our common purpose and unity day by day. On the other hand, we must forthrightly acknowledge that this school, this country, this Church is not God; it's imperfect; we need a constant reassessment and improvement, simply because our myth is embodied in — and by — professionally imperfect men and women.

The American Myth

Perhaps you can get a rough idea of the two extremes of near-blind naivete and near-blind cynicism — and the need to balance the two — if you consider the back-and-forth pendulum swing of the American myth in the last two generations.

In the 1940s, World War II embodied the American spirit about as perfectly as one could imagine: all those things we later celebrated about ourselves and our union on that truly moving — and too short-lived — Bicentennial, July 4, 1976. During that war, we all felt deeply that we were the living incarnation of the same aggressively generous spirit of liberty that impelled the heroes of Bunker Hill, the spirit of Washington and Jefferson and Lincoln. We were united in purpose against the

Germans and Japanese — who "perfectly" embodied the opposite spirit of tyranny and totalitarianism. We overlooked our flaws; we shared a common spirit and direction. The spirit of our myth and the embodiment of our myth were about as congruent as they could get, because the war forced us all, despite our differences, to put our total *faith* in our myth. America or world annihilation.

The symbols of our myth were charged with the power to move our hearts. In the war movies, "our" story was a story of striving against terrible odds; "our" boys — a Midwest farm boy, an Italian from California, a Jew from Manhattan, a WASP from Boston — all overcame their violent differences in boot camp, forged a single fighting unit, and went out there and did the job. Symbolic objects abounded: the flag stirred hearts, the national anthem brought us surging to our feet, service flags were proudly displayed in a family's front window: "We have a son in service; we're part of this, too!" The symbolic activities that showed our common purpose were armed service, work in defense plants, buying war bonds. There was even less griping about taxes during the war than in peace time.

It was a terrible, tragic time — yet an amazingly exhilarating time, too. We were one in purpose; the myth had become almost literally true. Of course it was too simplified, probably even naive, but that time and the ten years after the war are times we're all nostalgic for. It shows, again, in our movies. But when we were living them, we didn't even realize they were America's Golden Years — not until the pendulum swung completely the other way, from naivete to skepticism.

Then, twenty years after World War II, another war brought us nearly to the opposite, cynical extreme. Far from uniting us, the Vietnam War brought deep division. For many, at least at first, the myth continued to be idolized: If America was in a war, it must, by that very fact, be just — and we would win it, as if by some divine right. Gradually, a growing number became disillusioned, not only with the war but with the whole American myth. At the extreme, many lost "reverence" for the society's "sacred" symbols: Some refused to stand for the national anthem; some burned their draft cards and even burned the flag; some refused to pay all their taxes or to hold shares in companies that profited from the war. There was a deep division of spirit in the body of America between those who had lost their faith in the myth and those who still clung blindly to it.

That total reversal — that skepticism in the subconscious of the American myth-society, unthinkable during World War II — was closely related, I think, with one single "trigger-event": the assassination of President John F. Kennedy. Jack Kennedy was — or at least seemed at the time — the perfect embodiment of our myth: young, bright, forthright, confident, energetic, generous, classy, laughing. He gave us a good image of ourselves. In fact, while he was president, very few seemed troubled by our involvement in Vietnam (which, ironically, Kennedy had originated).

But then that day in November 1963, when he was senselessly slaughtered, it was as if the American myth he embodied had been slaughtered, too. I have never met a single person who was alive that day who can't remember precisely where he or she was at the moment the news was announced. So, it is difficult to explain even approximately to anyone who wasn't alive then what a soul-shattering event it was. The whole world — literally — came to a standstill. People went numb, glued to the television, as we learned that this great symbol had been annihilated by a pasty-faced nobody — who was then himself assassinated by the operator of a strip joint. The parallel and the contrast were obscene.

And then, one after another they came, the reminders that our myth was not only fallible but fragile: more assassinations, revelation of the American atrocities in Vietnam, the endless body counts, the deception of the Tonkin Gulf Resolution. Then Watergate and the revelation that, despite his protests, the president of the United States was an "unindicted co-conspirator" in a federal crime — and a liar. America was being run not as a myth but as a business. And the fallout from that ten years of disillusionment is still with us.

The Fallout

The shock of Kennedy's death and the seemingly endless series of disillusionments that followed it had a profound effect on the American soul: its myth. Those events spawned, if not cynicism, then at least a pervasive caution: "I'm not gonna get caught with my heart on my sleeve again!" Coupled with other developments — like rising crime in the streets, the rape of the ecology by greed, the pervasiveness of a cold, efficient technology — that hard-nosed defensiveness had a deadening effect on Americans' souls. What's more, the media, from the *New York Times* to the *National Enquirer,* seemed more than ever in our history to be focused on detecting the flaws in men and women who had formerly been "automatic heroes." The media, which during World War II, by common consent, never even showed President Roosevelt was a cripple, now told us the idolized Kennedy had been a womanizer, with shady connections to the Mob. Anyone who dares to raise a head above the crowd must now be ready to have every mistake of his or her life brought out for public scrutiny: drugs and alcohol, sexual improprieties, financial misconduct, even copying college papers.

A cynic might be tempted to suspect the *National Enquirer* has a team dogging the steps of Mother Teresa, knowing that, inevitably, she must have some dark secret in her past.

This skepticism is so pervasive that we — especially young people who have never known anything else — begin to take mistrust almost as a given. "Everybody's got an angle. Everybody's got skeletons in the closet. Play it cautious; play it cool. Keep your options open; don't get committed to anything; you'll get burned." That's called paranoia.

In such an atmosphere, it is quite difficult to "sell" a myth — even a relatively hole-free myth: honor ("Everybody cheats!"), chastity ("You're still a virgin?"), loyalty ("What my parents don't know won't hurt 'em"). It is virtually impossible to sell *faith* to a confirmed skeptic.

This skeptical fallout has contributed to (and been fed by) disillusionment about all kinds of sub-myths: the permanence of marriage, commitment to a cause, choosing a career that will benefit others rather than oneself, the dignity of a vocation as a priest or religious — all of which were unquestionably respected during the dark-rosy days of World War II. Now such vulnerability raises smiles of mild derision. All those commitments require faith, a self-giving without a money-back guarantee.

Perversely, the one segment of our lives that escapes the skepticism is the media themselves. Oh, we all know the commercials are a put-on, if not downright lies. But we still buy. We all know that news editors select what we see and read or don't, and the stories can be slanted in the telling to stress the management's point of view. But we still watch and listen, and our choices are affected by it. We all know that the people on "The Tonight Show" are only people just like us, who wake up with sour mouths in the morning. But don't we still believe, somewhere in our envious subconscious, that they — and what they say and do — are somehow "more important" than what we say and do, that they are "where it's *really* at?" We all know that Cosby and Alda and Burr are merely playing scripted characters. But don't we still, somewhere in our envious subconscious, resent the fact our doctors and fathers and lawyers aren't like that? We all know TV is in large part a crock. Yet, despite what we maintain when we talk about it, isn't there something inside us that falls for it? Almost as if something in us wanted, almost irresistibly, to be gullible? I wish someone could explain that to me.

There was a time when the words "our institutions" had a kind of solid grandness to them — our democratic government, our banking system, our educational enterprise. An "institution" is, after all, merely another word for the concrete apparatus by which our convictions — our myths — are worked out in our everyday lives. But now all institutions fall under the almost universal suspicion. The institution is "them," not "us." And nowhere is that more evident than with the institutional Church.

The Skeptical Fallout and Today's Institutional Church

Concurrent with the massive change in attitudes in secular America in the last two decades, the Catholic Church committed "herself" to a profound change of her own attitudes. Before Vatican II, the Church had been a quite formidable and unbending and enclosed institution. With the advent of the breezy Pope John XXIII, she decided to "open the windows," not only to have more meaningful effect on the world she was dedicated to evangelize, but also to let the world have (at least some kind of) input into the Church's understanding of herself. As a result, a Catholic who died in 1960 and came back to life today would be in for one big surprise! He or she would quite likely not even recognize the Church.

But many other changes came about not as a result of the pronouncements of Vatican II, but rather as a result of the Church's new openness to the world and to change. The Church and her members are no less susceptible to the prevailing skepticism and the resulting hesitancy to pledge oneself to any act of faith or any permanent commitment.

Priests and nuns and even bishops rejecting the commitment of their vows became so commonplace that it ceased to be newsworthy. The official Church censures theologians for expressing views on sexuality that many of the still-faithful also believe to be true, and societies of eminent theologians defend their colleague against the censure, and again in the public press. Public surveys indicate 80 percent of church-going Catholics practice artificial birth control. Bishops differ publicly with one another over recommending condoms as a lesser evil than the danger of AIDS. Priests are arrested for soliciting sex with children. Many in the Church, from professors of theology to high school students, find it difficult not to judge at least the leadership of the Church to be chauvinist, when it judges women unfit candidates for the priesthood, or even the diaconate. Talented and persuasive professors — even in Catholic colleges — belittle the naivete of faith or even the existence of a transcendent dimension of human life.

The effect is cumulative, even though the reader picks up one item here, one item there, even though the effect is not conscious but subconscious. It's enough to baffle a professional theologian, much more the man or woman in the pews who left "all those big questions" back in college, and even more an adolescent who, by the very nature of adolescence, is questioning *all* his or her childhood myths and who has been far more affected by the pervasive skepticism than his or her parents and grandparents — who were born when faith, trust, and commitment were not necessarily such suspect positions.

At least it seems, as William Butler Yeats wrote, "The center cannot hold." As a more practical materialist might put it: "When the management's at odds with itself, don't invest."

And yet, astonishingly — perhaps miraculously — people do maintain their commitment to the institutional Church. After the exodus of the past two decades, the organized religions in America are actually showing slight but gradual gains in their active memberships.

Part of the reason for the return of many "fallen-away" Catholics, as we saw with the "saints" of the Rocker myth who destroyed themselves, is that the myths the disaffected chose to substitute for religion simply didn't do the job. They tried to compel casual sex — or art, psychedelic drugs, getting to the top, crusading for causes — to fulfill that inner human need for a numinous power, for a profound enrichment of the human spirit. And it just didn't work, simply because — whether those goals or activities are objectively good or bad or indifferent in themselves — none of them, nor all of them together, have it within themselves to deliver that kind of enduring conviction of personal worth, to fulfill that primal need.

As my student Wally Kuhn said, "All the boats leak. You've got to find the one that leaks least." And those boats — those myths like sex, art, causes, etc. — just have too many leaks to carry one's whole meaning very far.

Part of the reason, however, is also that the people who remained in the Church and the people who returned to the Church found that they did have a felt need to express, communally and publicly, their gratitude to the God who opened the door to it all. Of course they could have gone off and worshiped God alone in the woods, just as a couple could go off alone in the woods and declare their marriage vows. But, for them, that wasn't enough. And they found that, no matter what her faults or how blatant, the Roman Catholic Church is "home."

As Peter, also a renegade for awhile but our first pope, said, "Lord, to whom shall we go? You have the words of eternal life." The primal joy of faith.

That sense of a lifelong tribal "belonging" is far more right-brain intuitive than a coldly analytical scrutiny of the hard facts, but it isn't to be sold short for that. Your loyalty to your own family, to your friends, to your school — despite their obvious flaws — is no more logically reasoned than such Catholics' loyalty to a myth and an institution that "feel right" to them. The logical analysis, the kind of business you have to engage in to justify that loyalty to non-believers or to want-to-believers, will have to wait for later chapters.

The Need for a Director

As I develop this perhaps overdeveloped analogy, try to fathom as it proceeds what insights it has to offer the Church — or any other institutionalization of an ideal.

One year, a group of seniors and juniors wanted to start a lacrosse team at our school. They had a tremendous amount of spirit, too much to want that spirit dampened by all the fuss about coaches and moderators and captains. They'd just "get together," they said, every afternoon, united by the common enthusiasm for the game and for one another. Well, there were dentists' appointments. And detention. And disagreements — about how long practices should run, and who should play what position, and how long each player should stay in the game. It all lasted a little less than two weeks. Spirit alone isn't enough to keep the body together. There's got to be a head.

Or consider the late-night reruns of Mickey Rooney and Judy Garland movies (from the simpler days of World War II). The kids are sitting around lamenting that they have nothing to do, or pondering how they'll raise some improbable sum for their dog's operation, when suddenly one of them gets a brilliant idea! There's practically a light bulb flashing in each eye. "Hey, you guys! We could put on . . . a *show!*" The enthusiasm, the spirit, the dedication are infectious. And off they go, in all directions at once. And everybody just "falls into" the right parts and the right offstage jobs, and nobody argues or tries to hog the stage. The only opposition comes from outside: sudden illness, a group of jealous kids, the old grump who won't let them use his barn. And after overcoming all those obstacles, it's opening night, and the show's a *dazzler!* Now that's the only place enthusiasm can carry it off with no interference from an authority who has the last word: the movies. After directing seventy plays, with teenagers and with adults, I can testify without hesitation it just won't work — *especially* with adults.

A congregation is a body without a spirit; all discipline and no spirit or enthusiasm. A community is, ideally, an enspirited group of people; most of the power comes from below. But a community without *any* discipline — Judy and Mickey to the contrary — is, in the real world, only one thing: chaos.

You can't have every player calling the plays; we all bump into one another. When you do a show, either a director is imposed, or chosen by vote, or beats everybody else up — or there's no show. Somebody has to know the script better than the cast or at least has the power to say that, even though no one is quite sure the best way to do such-and-such, "This is the way we're gonna do it," or nobody does anything.

In a play, there are only two organizing-disciplining factors: the script and the director. The script usually asks the actors to stay more or less within fixed dialogue and action and place, but the movements and intonations and unscripted motivations are left pretty much up to the director and actors. There is one script of *Hamlet* that is normative. But there have been old, young, Elizabethan, modern, and even female Hamlets. A good script, then, is both normative and flexible.

Now, some directors are very strict; they have the whole show mapped out to the tiniest inflection of voice in their own skulls, and they work the actors and technicians to death until that ideal is actually embodied on stage or on film. (Hitchcock worked that way.) With unskilled actors, that's just about the only way to go. It's the "style" of direction that has to be used at summer camps and the lower grades of school.

Other directors, especially with more experienced actors and technicians, will be freer; they sketch out the overall plan and the "values" they want to stress, but then allow a lot of input from the members. Such directors trust their people, even to the point of allowing an actor to experiment and improvise (at least for awhile), in order to stretch the heretofore supposed limits laid down by the script and the director's vision of the play.

More than the director, each actor has a far more intense interest in his or her own role, more time to probe the ins and outs of the character and his or her purpose in the play, and more knowledge of what he or she can and cannot do as an actor. Ideally, the actor works out the part, talks it over with the director, and, again ideally, the whole thing is enriched by many viewpoints and insights and skills. The director has the last word, but he or she doesn't have the last idea. Like the best scripts, the best directors are normative but flexible.

However, lest we forget, no matter what "original sin" really means, human beings are selfish. The walk-on with one line just itches to stretch it to two. At least. The leads want to dominate; the chorus "knows its place" but doesn't exactly like it. No matter how much more experienced the director is, more than a few first-timers are certain they could do it better. That's how revolutions are made.

This long (seeming) digression is an attempt to show the honest and open (and sometimes painful) give-and-take that differentiates a real community from some kind of let's-get-the-job-done-and-get-out-of-here congregation. It shows the difference between a truly communitarian Church (or nation, or school), where people trust one another (without being gullible), and a Church built on power and fear, which has no more soul than a machine, and which is merely tolerated for the self-interest of the individualists of which it is composed.

In this protracted analogy, the "script" is the scriptures, or the Constitution, the job contract, or the school catalogue. The "director" is the official Church, or the present government, or the manager, or the school administration. They can interpret the script as they will, but, in fairness to the author, only insofar as the present interpretation doesn't violate the author's intention. They can lean more strongly toward authoritarianism when their "actors" are young and inexperienced. But after that, directors are in danger of underestimating the talent and experiences of those they are directing. They could well be insulting their actors, to say nothing of impoverishing themselves, producing a work far less good than the director alone could envision.

The "actors" are the Church members, or citizens, or workers, or faculty and students. Each one has a greater knowledge of the *particulars,* while the director has a broader understanding of the *whole* operation. If either the director, or the actors, or any single actor "wins," then they all lose.

The only key to a communitarian enterprise is a commodity not much in evidence today: trust — not only the actors' trust of the director, but the director's trust of the actors. Each "side" has to have the confidence (in oneself) and the trust (in the others) at least to suggest that a mistake has been made. Trouble is, directors often feel their control is being threatened, and actors begin to think whatever comments they have will never be heard.

Without trust, without both freedom and discipline, many plays — and churches, and families, and schools — keep on going, but are really failures, at least in actually embodying what they claim to embody. Sad, because it doesn't have to be that way.

~ Questions for Discussion ~

1. The chapter makes a strong — perhaps too strong — case that there is a pervasive skepticism in America today, a show-me-first attitude, and a reluctance to trust any individual or institution until there's an iron-clad guarantee. What evidence do you have in your own life that would negate — or at least soften — the chapter's thesis?

2. The chapter also makes a strong case regarding the greater difficulty in being a practicing Catholic today than in the simpler days of the 1940s and 1950s. What evidence do you see — in your own family, your parish, your school — that there might be hope for the old Church, that the tide might be turning?

3. The latter part of the chapter dealt extensively with the analogy between creating a play and creating a real-though-imperfect Church. If the comparison is valid, how should it change your own personal way of dealing with the institutional Church — pastor, bishop, Vatican?

Chapter 4

Who's Got the "Right" God?

SO FAR, we've talked almost exclusively about us: How self-protective isolation or insulation cramps our lives, our need for union with others and for some kind of personal and communal "plan": a myth — which gives us direction and purpose and against which we can judge whether we're doing the job well or falling behind. Now it's time to bring God into that net of relationships. Like other societies, a religious society has a horizontal dimension of union with the other members, but, unlike them, a religious society also has a vertical dimension of union with God. In fact, God is the very root of their union together.

The question in the title of this chapter, at least as it is phrased, is of course absurd. Yet many people get the cockeyed idea that Moslems have "their" God, and pagans had "their" gods, and *we* have "the one true God," and so forth. Almost like an enormous shell game, where only one shell covers the real pea, the real picture of God, and all the other shells are completely empty. No. There is a very real portrait (not photograph) of the One God under each of the shells, the same Subject, but painted by artists with very different styles and viewpoints.

There is only one Mind Behind It All, and each great philosophy and world religion is trying to "capture" God as well as it can. Each myth system tries to do the same thing: express in human — therefore imperfect — terms the nature of an Entity who is beyond all but the most remote human comprehension.

God exists inside time and space, but also *outside* time and space. God "ante-dated time"; God "takes up no space" — and yet is greater than the universe. God is unlimited by space/time; we, on the contrary, are pretty much locked into space/time (though not totally). All we say is conditioned by the fact our minds are "space/time oriented." Our minds get disoriented when we get out "into God." As humans, we need something to "hold on to."

It's not just God who poses us those problems. We have the same problem with earthbound realities that are not material but that are nonetheless "there": love, honor, truth, and so forth. Our space/time minds twist to deal with the God-Entity — just as they must wrench to "envision" curved space or positrons moving backward in time. Just as our eyes will never work fast enough to catch an atom, they'll never work fast enough to catch God. The problem's not with atoms or with God; the problem's with the way our eyes are made. And (although I hate to admit it), I find it difficult to describe, even so-so, things I *can* see.

So religions have tried to "capture" God, even in an inadequate way, in concrete pictures: an Old Man on a white throne, a dancing woman with many arms, "a Person made of light." We need some way to "focus" this Entity who is, by God's very nature, unfocusable. (Jews and Moslems, on the contrary, forbid *any* attempt to image God, lest the image *become* God: an idol.)

That's a humbling fact, that God always escapes — almost totally — any net of words or pictures we attempt to throw around him. Perhaps an experience I had might make it clearer. One day I was walking along a country road, just sort of "hanging out" with God, when along came a black Labrador retriever with a stick in her mouth. She wanted me to throw the stick, so, obediently, I did. But after awhile, my arm gave out, so I stopped throwing the stick. Well, that Lab was pretty put out. She came up and bumped me with her butt, and she looked up at me with a bitchy look. "Don't you know your job? Get on with it!" And I replied (out loud, I confess), "Wait a minute, kiddo. You're a *dog,* and I'm a *person!*" And right there I had an insight — what James Joyce called "an epiphany": that nice Lab understood my thoughts and purposes and nature just about as well as I understand God's thoughts and purposes and nature.

Humbling. But if it's the truth, we must bow to it — as we do to the unpleasant truths of death and trips to the dentist.

Nevertheless, God is not utterly unknowable. I can find out things about God by looking at God's work — the universe and all that's in it, including the human mind and soul. And I can find out things about God by my experience with him/her — including my unpleasant experiences, like trying to make sense of why God let a seventeen-year-old friend get cancer and die. And I can find out things about God by praying — centering into my soul and connecting into the Mind Behind It All. But just as a husband can't say he's got his wife "all figured out," I can't say I've got God "all figured out," no matter how long I live with God.

Therefore, the statements of all philosophies and religions about God — their scriptures, their dogmas, their theologies — are all inadequate to their Subject. What's more, they are not only *humanly* limited but they are also *culturally* limited: restricted to what was known about the world and human beings at the particular time in history when the statements were made.

Thus, the author of Genesis, for instance, wrote as if the earth were the center of the whole material universe, covered with a crystal-bowl firmament — simply because that's all *anybody* at the time knew about cosmology. Perhaps the reason Jesus didn't "ordain" any women at the Last Supper was that, *in his culture,* a woman priest was totally unacceptable, if not even "unthinkable." Until Vatican II, it was culturally "unthinkable" that the Roman Catholic Church's customs and symbols could be anything else but *European* customs and symbols.

No statements about God — in fact no religion — are without room for improvement. Our common Subject is, after all, infinite, and we are finite. "All the boats leak."

The Goldilocks Method

Goldilocks found what she wanted by testing: one bed too soft, one too hard, one "just right." Not quite your analytical scientific method, but reasonable, at least for a start.

What follows is not a comprehensive study of each great philosophy and world religion. If it were, you couldn't afford to buy the book. Or lift it. It is a quick sketch so that, if one God-view seems to "feel right" to you (even though it doesn't appeal to me), you can find more about it in an encyclopedia, and if it still looks good, pursue it further.

What's more, I can deal with the God-views only from *my* quite limited perspective. I don't mean they are limited by my being Christian — or even a Catholic and a priest. (In fact, it's because I find the other views lacking that I *am* a Christian, rather than the other way round.) I mean the brief treatments that follow are limited by *my* experience of God — in studying the universe, especially the human mind and soul, in my experience of the way God has dealt with me and people I know, and in my praying. Like any of the great religious myths, my own religious myth is limited by my experience. Thus, I deal here with the major God-views as honestly as I can, given the limitations of page-space, but I deal also with why they seem, to *me,* not quite "right," inadequate at least to my personal experience of God.

In my experience, God is both transcendent (beyond the limits) and immanent (within the limits).

"Transcendent" is a fairly common word to describe the "Fifth Dimension," a way of existing that ante-dated time and that is unlimited by space. Again, even in thinking about the transcendent, we are limited by space/time vision, and find ourselves thinking of God "way out there," as if the Fifth Dimension were light-years away, behind a thin membrane that separates the physical universe from the non-physical heaven.

Oddly enough, understanding the transcendent dimension to reality depends on the same skills of imagination that are necessary to understand modern physics — which is why you were never given an explanation of God more adult than an Old Man till your mind was able to cope with such things as modern physics.

Somehow we manage to suspend our disbelief when we try to imagine that the chair we are sitting on right now — which is solid enough to keep us from dropping to the floor — is not really solid at all, but actually a whirlwind of atoms. It takes a similar suspension of disbelief to imagine that there is a Fifth Dimension that spreads all through what we understand to be reality (the universe) but extends *beyond* the four dimensions we can measure: length, width, thickness — and time. But, if there is a God who ante-dated time and created space, then there must be such a dimension to reality, even though we can't see it.

Similarly, no one can see your soul — your inner self, your who-I-am. They see only your body and take educated guesses about your invisible soul. But it's there, although even you can't see it. Your soul is also a transcendent entity, ultimately independent of space and time and death.

"Immanent" (locked inside) is often confused with "imminent" (just about to happen) and even "eminent" (lofty). Rather, "immanent" means "right down inside"; your soul is immanent in your body. In my experience, God is not *only* beyond space and time but also "here and now." It's as if God were inside the universe exactly the way your soul is inside your body — energizing it and yet able in a very real sense to be free of it.

I am aware of God's presence when I pray, and God is not spatially distant but as close to me as my own inner self. As the psychiatrist Carl Jung suggests, it's quite likely God speaks to us through the (invisible but real) subconscious.

I also "sense" (there's no better word) a kind of "presence" in nature and art and people, what I referred to earlier as the "numinous." When I'm alone by a lake and the sky is ablaze with uncountable stars, when I stand in front of Michelangelo's David, when I see a man or woman who has performed some heroic act "beyond-it-all," I find myself saying, "Oh, my God!" And I can't help but believe my instinctive response has been absolutely right.

Therefore, in explaining the major God-views, some seem to "restrict" God too much, making God too transcendent, too unapproach-able, or making God too immanent, too locked into creation. Those judgments may differ from your experience. It's only a sketch you can amplify at your leisure and your pleasure.

The Too-Immanent God

Pagans and pantheists equate God with what God created, leaving out any transcendent dimension beyond time and space.

Pagans believed the god lived *within* the waterfall. The lightning and thunder and seas were god-filled. The life-source of the grain was a god. Pagans, with admirable humility, saw gods everywhere they turned. As time went on, civilizations all over the earth, independently of one another, began to see these powers not only as personal, with capricious wills, but as persons. The god of thunder was a cranky old man; the goddess of grain was gentle and lovely; the god of fire and tools was an ugly hunchback. And there was one god in charge (a male, "of course") because somebody had to keep this society of gods in line.

Because the divine powers were within matter, the witch doctor could manipulate the gods by manipulating matter. The gods could be "fo-cused" into symbols — the sacred tree, the totem pole, the rock — but quite often the signpost became an idol, a god in its own right. (Thus Jews and Moslems forbid symbols of God.)

Paganism may seem to us crude. Yet pagans have something to tell us, in our technological paradise, where neon and tall buildings and sophis-tication wall out the numinous from our lives. Pagans knew instinctively what Jesus meant when he said, "Unless you become as little children, you will never encounter God."

But my intelligence tells me that, if God created the powers of the universe, God has to be not only greater than they are but independent of them. And my experience tells me, beyond the slightest doubt, that God cannot be manipulated. After half a century of trying everything short of sacrificing a virgin, there is no truth before which I am humbler than that one.

Pantheism believes all things *are* God, trapped inside matter. Just as the later pagans smashed the one Power into lots of little god-lets, pan-theists smash God even further: everything we see in the universe is God — or at least "filled with God." Romantic philosophers and po-ets saw "Nature" itself as divine. Like pagans, pantheists have a healthy sense of the numinous.

The most philosophically sophisticated pantheism is Buddhism, although if you study it more carefully than we can here, you will find that Buddhism defies easy pigeon-holing. At times, because its "God" — the Life-Force — seems so totally impersonal, it is hard even to be sure that it *is* a religion, if you regard "religion" as having do with our personal relationship to a personal God. You can't really have a relationship with an impersonal entity, and thus some critics even consider Buddhism an atheism.

For Buddhists, wherever there is life, there is God. To kill any living thing — fleas, snakes, cows — is an act of blasphemy, a kind of deicide. That animal carries, within its degrading flesh, the same divine life a human being enjoys.

Buddhists believe that the flesh "degrades" the spirit imprisoned within it. Flesh does that by engendering *desire* — for impossible dreams, for a different world, for health instead of sickness. So, since there is always a gap between what is and what we desire, that gap *is* suffering. Thus, to get rid of the suffering, we have to subject the rebellious flesh to the control of the inner soul, willing the self to reject desire and thus to reject the suffering desire generates. Once the devotee achieves "Enlightenment," Nirvana, all barriers between the Life-Force in ourselves and the Life-Force in all the living things disappear, as we are "blended into" them. One merges with the Oversoul.

As I said before, I have learned a great deal from Buddhism, especially about communicating with God. And I have no trouble accepting the futility of many of our desires as the cause of much of our unhappiness. Nor would I question the connection between aggressive selfishness and crime or between defensive self-centeredness and withered lives. But I have a great deal of problem with the Buddhists' theory — though perhaps that is due to the overly left-brain conditioning of my "Western" mind.

The cause of my disquiet is at the very "heart" of the Buddhist philosophy: the gradual, painstaking negation of the individual. When the merger with the Oversoul is complete, like a bucket of water tipped into the ocean, the individual ceases to have any "self." This is not a union, at least as a Western mind would conceive it, as in a family union. This is absorption. No room for love, since love can occur only where two individuals freely surrender to one another and still remain each a self.

My other difficulty with Buddhism is its negative attitude toward the world — not "the World" as St. Paul uses it: the wickedness and corruption of moral evil — but the world I spoke of before, which makes me say, "Oh, my God!" Here is where the Buddhists part company with their more romantic fellow pantheists: they see God imprisoned in matter and degraded by it; the romantics (and I) see God energizing matter and radiating from it.

Chesterton put my problem better — and more concretely. All the statues of Buddhist saints have their eyes closed. But all saints in Christian churches have their eyes wide open — sometimes to a degree defying belief. To achieve Nirvana ("Nothingness"), the Buddhist shuts out the world. Everything in the world is merely a distraction from the painful process of — at least as I see it — homogenizing reality into one all-absorptive All. I may be wrong in rejecting it, but it "feels" out of kilter.

The Too-Transcendent God

Whereas the pagan and the pantheist see a God I find to be too embodied in the physical world and too limited to it, Deists and the Platonists find the Mind Behind It All too disembodied from the physical world and too unconcerned with it. As with Buddhists, one is tempted to think (perhaps unfairly) the Deist view springs as much from a profound distaste for the world and human beings as from a profound respect for God. The world in general is so nasty that God couldn't dirty his pure "hands" with it.

Deists, like all believers in God, recognize the necessity for an intelligent Cause behind such a miraculously well-organized universe. But they believe God — being inexpressibly perfect and unable to "soil" himself — simply started the enterprise rolling and then walked away. If God is so "distant," then, we can have no person-to-Person experience of him, except very indirectly through the "footprints" God has left on creation. We can marvel at God, but God is no more accessible to us than an artist who has died.

But that is, very obviously, in direct contradiction to my own experience — and the experience of millions of others. There is a difference in my awe at the star-flocked sky and my awe at Michelangelo's David. True, in both I marvel at the artistry, and when I marvel at the David, I marvel not only at the artist, Michelangelo, who designed it, but I marvel also at the Artist who designed the artist, Michelangelo. And yet in dealing with God-the-Artist, I genuinely believe I am *communing* with the Artist, not in some head-trip, aesthetical way, but person-to-Person.

Very basically, *Platonists* believe the objects we experience in the world are only inept copies of their otherworldly originals. (Notice how many philosophies try to get God off the hook for creating creatures as obviously imperfect as human beings.) The real ideas exist beyond the physical world, in a transcendent and perfect state — in the Mind of God. Thus, there are three meanings to the word "idea" *(logos):* the Idea of any reality in the Mind of God, the idea programmed by God into the physical object, and the highly imperfect idea of that nature grasped by a human mind. Human minds, in their imperfectly realized state, wrongly believe what they see is "it." But, as Plato tells us in his parable "The Cave," what we see are merely shadows — of imitations — of Reality.

There is much to be said about Plato's vision of reality — especially about the arrogance with which we say our ideas and dogmas have "the last word" about anything. And early Christians, moving out of an initially Jewish way of thinking into a Greek way of thinking, found much in Platonism to help them "translate" the Jewish gospel to a Greek mind-set.

But in being so complimentary to God, Platonists (to my mind) end up being too uncomplimentary to what God created. Praise for God, but not much praise for God's skill — or purpose — as a creator. God made humans imperfect for a *purpose:* so they could evolve.

Not only is the God of the Deists and Platonists too "far away" but also too impersonal to account for the experiences of the Immanentists. Our experience has revealed not only an intense and personal *presence,* but also a loving concern, quite contrary to the picture of a self-absorbed Inventor of Toys, who leaves them behind when they no longer fascinate, a God who seems to have no more personality than a perfect right triangle. (Oddly, whoever designed the one-dollar bill must have looked at God that way: an unblinking Eye at the top of a pyramid.)

The Balance: The Immanent-Transcendent God

At least for me, pagans and pantheists limit God too severely by locking God within our way of existing: the union of God with creatures is eventually not a family with their Father, but an absorption into the Creator of the energy God "mistakenly" dissipated into matter. Deists and Platonists, on the other hand, seem to limit God too severely by locking God *out* of creation. The relation between God and creatures seems no more real than the "relation" between a toymaker and the toys he has put up for sale.

Each extreme does, however, account for half of what I've experienced of God. The immanence of God — God's nearness (the stars over the lake) — is sometimes positively frightening; and yet God's transcendence — God's refusal to be answerable to *me* (my mother's endless years of dying) — are both facts of my experience. Therefore, any description of God that fails to account for *both* immanence and transcendence is only half an answer — for me.

The only two myth-systems that combine the two are the basic insights of Judaism and Christianity (not the various sects of the two, just the basic insights). In Judaism, God is so transcendent — so "Other" — that you are not even allowed to pronounce God's real name out loud or write it. And yet "God's House" is at the center of our town; God dwells in our midst. In Christianity, God literally "was made flesh and pitched his tent among us."

I freely confess my bias. On the one hand, I don't want a God so transcendent he doesn't give a damn what I do. On the other, I don't want a God so immanent and buddy-buddy that he lays down no rules-of-the-game, forgives any mistake without any need for me to apologize to the One Who Opened the Door. Both the too-far-away God and the one-of-the-guys God end up making what I do with my life, good or bad, nothing but an irrelevance.

That is what *I* want: a God who cares, but a God who is not a patsy. But the question remains: *Why* do I want that kind of God? Surely not because it makes it easier for me. Easier if God were utterly transcendent and couldn't care less about my stupidities; easier if God were utterly immanent and able to be distracted with a virgin here and there. But something inside me wants a God demanding yet merciful, beyond my bribes yet susceptible to my trusting service, inexpressibly holy yet — unthinkably — my Friend.

Is that the God of my wishful thinking? Or is that the God who allowed me to live in order to find just such a contrary God?

It's an interesting question.

~ Questions for Discussion ~

1. Tackle that final interesting question. Just as you have an ideal self — a character — you want to live up to, you also have an idea of God. What evidence do you have from your experience that would indicate your idea of God is not merely a mental fabrication (like a unicorn or Santa Claus) but rather an inadequate-but-serviceable picture of what God is really like (like your assessment of your best friend's inner self)? What hard evidence do you have that God is not your own personal creation?

2. Of necessity, the chapter was able to explore the nature of God only from my own limited perspective. What are your own experiences of God? If you can make at least a rough estimate of a person's inner self — his or her "character" and "personality" — then you should be able to get some sense of God's personality from the way God made the universe, from the way God's acted with you and with people you know, and from your own praying.

What insights do you get into God's nature from the way the planets are made and the way they interact? What insights from the fact of an eons-long evolution, from the rise upward from rock to rutabaga to rabbit to men and women, from the recurrence of seasons — each year the same and yet each year unique? What insights from the way human beings are made: body, mind, soul? What insights from the ways God inspires, challenges, thwarts — and hurts — you and the people you know? (I doubt God steps in each time and pulls the trigger, but God is ultimately responsible for a universe in which unexpected pain can happen.) Finally, if you're not still too shy to talk about it, what have you learned about God from talking to him person-to-Person?

Chapter 5

The First People of God

GOD REVEALS HIS NATURE, his personality, his character in the natures he has created: in the order and surprise of the universe, in the patient (and highly inefficient) evolution of life here on earth, in the bipolar balance of the analytical-intuitive human brain. But God also reveals himself in patterns of habitual behavior with people — and peoples. And one of the most privileged and pogrom-plagued histories has been that of the Jewish people. Their experience of God is a treasury of insight for any human being, but particularly for a Christian, since Jesus rose out of Israel, and it is impossible to understand him, except in a very surface way, without some understanding of the lifeview — the myth — out of which he came.

The Hebrew Mind

In a marvelously precarious way, the Hebrews balanced the transcendent and immanent relationship between God and humankind.

On the one hand, Yahweh is so transcendently holy that Job is silenced in his questioning by a sudden realization of who God is in comparison to who Job himself is — a Whirlwind in comparison to one man's breath. The place where Moses meets Yahweh is so sanctified that Moses emerges from it, face blazing with light. Yahweh's true name, *ehyeh asher ehyeh* (I Am Who Am), is so powerful that no Hebrew can even speak it; no Hebrew can say even "I am."

And yet, on the other hand, Hebrews also have a very down-to-earth relationship with that same Yahweh. They bridge the gulf between Platonic distance and pagan materialism, speaking of God in very anthropomorphic terms — as if God is as human as they themselves. They talk as if God has eyes, mouth, hands; feels joy, hatred, anger, love; God speaks, hears, even whistles Adam and Eve to walk with him in the Garden; God sits companionably and chats with Abraham and Sarah; Jacob even wrestles with God!

And yet this is not just a Middle Eastern version of the Greek Olympian gods. For one thing Yahweh is One-of-a-Kind; there is no other power worthy of the name "God." For another, unlike the Greek gods, who were capricious, fickle, and downright eccentric, Yahweh is rigorously consistent and relentlessly loyal. But most important is that the Hebrews know that their anthropomorphism is only a way of *talking* about Yahweh. It is clear that their God is within history, but God is immeasurably beyond history, too, and independent of it.

The people who embodied their experience of God in the Old Testament were very definitely not a "head-trip" people. They surely seemed to delight in framing laws, fine-tuning them down to the last microscopic detail. But they seemed to have little time for theorizing — theses, careful definition of terms, and step-by-step logic — as the Greeks were. That is not to say they were not intelligent or rational; far from it. But their dealings with God, as manifested in their scriptures, are far more person-to-Person than mind-to-Problem. If Greek thinking about the Mind Behind It All is more comfortable with concepts, with the left-brain, with the "head," Hebrew thinking about God is more comfortable with symbols, with the right-brain, with the "heart." Plato played chess with God; Jacob wrestled with him.

For the Hebrew, in fact, every non-physical reality — words, ideas, spirits, God — was a lot more "solid" than our sophisticated, at times even airy, concepts. When someone spoke a word, it *materialized.* It is merely God's word that triggers creation; once someone has "given his word," as Isaac did to Jacob, it's out there; there is no taking it back. A person's word — his or her name — had "heft." It was a pledge of fidelity, even more binding than a son or daughter given as hostage. A person's word also revealed his or her function in the community; to change a person's name was to change the job he or she did for the community (for instance, changing the name "Simon" to *Petros,* "rock"). And according to the New Testament, Jesus is God's Word: not only the expression of his self, but his pledge.

For the Hebrew, the object of analytical "theology" was inseparable from intuitive "praying." How could you make statements about God without communicating with God? How could you speak about God as if he were some colorless "Entity," like "The Uncaused First Cause"? The object of theology is to know God better, and there is no better way to know any person — even the transcendent/immanent Yahweh — than to go on a long journey with that person. And that is the history/theology of the Hebrew people.

History as Homily

Anyone who approaches the Hebrew Scriptures, the Old Testament, expecting a scrupulously researched and footnoted historical record is either insane or crazy. And yet, at one extreme, sophisticates (Scientism) approach the Old Testament as if it were no more than a pleasant diversion in peasant folklore, and, at the other extreme, simplicists (Fundamentalism) approach it as if it were a documentary movie, shot on the spot.

Either approach misses the whole point, in a truly mindless way; no matter in which extreme you're tempted to miss the point. A book like *The Color Purple* is *neither* a mere afternoon's entertainment, like an espionage novel, nor is it a historical record of one actual woman's rising from servitude to selfhood. *The Color Purple* is a myth: not a literal, historical record, but a story that tells more truth about women than any left-brain, analytical study of female psychology I've ever encountered.

In the same way, the books of Genesis, Exodus, Judges, and so forth surely cannot be held for downs on historical accuracy the way, say, a modern history of World War II could. To misread them in that way — either to mock their naivete, or to cast their dates in stone — is more an indictment of the mental capacities of those passing judgment than of the scriptures themselves.

A great deal of the Hebrew Scriptures is historically true; there is archeological evidence to back it up, just as there is archeological evidence to back up the stories of the Trojan War and the theory of evolution. But a great deal of it is legend, used to make a point, just as the legend of St. Christopher (who probably never existed) can be used to make a very valid point: the same point as the story of the Good Samaritan. To those who know the Hebrew Scriptures only from biblical movies (and not from a full reading of the books themselves) the entire Old Testament is limited to only one book: Exodus (Moses) and perhaps a few ill-remembered psalms from Sunday Mass ("My shepherd is the Lord . . . "). On the contrary, it is filled with short stories, poems, collections of proverbs, law books, violent prophetic speeches — lots of those. But few people who have an opinion of the Old Testament have ever really read it, not unlike people who pooh-pooh pop music without ever giving it a fair hearing.

And even the movie versions of Exodus are more hoked-up than any book of the scriptures. In the movies, Moses is the barrel-chested Charlton Heston: intrepid, stalwart, articulate. In the actual book, he's more like Don Knotts: dithering, terrified, tongue-tied. In fact, most of the "heroes" Yahweh chose were anything but Arthurian knights! (And from the heroes he chose, you can get a *great* insight into Yahweh's personality: the kinds of things God likes and doesn't.) Adam and Eve, for starters: washouts. Noah: a drunken eccentric. Abraham and Sarah: the perfect choice for the grandparents of all Hebrews, right? Childless, both in their nineties, and barren as a pair of bricks. General Gideon: the victorious coward. For a contender against Goliath, the first person you'd think of is a spindly shepherd kid named David and not his eleven Arnold Schwarzenegger brothers. God's idea of a hero is different from ours.

The stories of the Old Testament are trying to reveal truth, not as today's professional historians try to document events, but trying to find the *significance* in events. The authors of the Hebrew scriptures were not reporters; they were commentators. "What does this event mean for the future? What mistakes does it tell us we've been making? What's Yahweh trying to tell us about the consequences of our wrong choices?"

Take a case in point. My trust in the Old Testament would not be threatened in any way if I were to find out that, on a particular day, at a particular hour, Abraham did not actually drag his son Isaac onto a pile of wood and prepare to cut his son's throat. To say with the sophisticate that the story is utter fabrication is to say that "Jack and the Beanstalk" has nothing to tell us about male sexuality. At the other extreme, to say with the simplicist that it actually did occur historically is to say that at one time beans actually *did* sprout into stalks that went "right up to the sky!"

The story of Abraham and Isaac, like any story out of Aesop, never happened, but it nonetheless tells a timeless truth: Often, without our even realizing, we turn the things we love into idols, more important than God.

Unlike movies, I am not locked into actually seeing a fire-ball cut a pair of tablets out of the rock and burning into them ten indecipherable words. Whether the Ten Commandments were carved in granite — or shale, or parchment, or never carved at all — is hardly the point. People spend so much time demythologizing or deifying the method by which Yahweh communicated them that they forget the whole point: the message. And the message is no more than what an intelligent person could find out for his or her self, reflecting on the human programming: you were created, therefore revere God; all the others around you are as human as you are, therefore treat them as you would yourself.

All the grumbles and mayhem we get from the God of biblical movies has very little to do with even the admitted excesses we find in the Hebrew Scriptures, most of which, even when they do occur, are — as in the movies — hardly the point of the story, but merely "special effects" to keep the audience awake.

To someone who has read the entire story of Israel's experience with Yahweh, Isaiah's terror at being in the presence of the transcendent God, a man of unclean lips from a people of unclean lips, is balanced by the immanent God in the book of Hosea and in the Song of Songs, where God is a faithful and passionate husband to his wife. And in *quite* explicit terms! Yahweh, for instance, speaking of Israel: "My beloved's breasts are like two fauns that feed among the lilies."

As a result, the response of the Hebrew to Yahweh was neither the fawning of the pagan nor the aloofness of the Deist, not deadly formal, nor merely liturgical, but *personal.* The Hebrew believed that any worship or prayer — or theologizing — without personal involvement is, by that very fact, hypocritical.

The Hebrews and the Personality of God

For the Jew, God is not some characterless "Energy" somewhere "out there." God is involved personally in human history. However primitive the early Hebrew mind might have been, the Hebrews' God was not locked within Nature, nor a distant Uncaused First Cause, but rather a God revealed — unclearly but concretely — in dealings with them. Their everyday struggles against their own baser instincts were a microcosm of Yahweh's cosmic struggle against Chaos. Too simply to be sure, the early Hebrews saw a direct connection between moral evil (sin) and physical evil (plague, famine, foreign invasion); an individual or the whole Hebrew nation could, by their sins, "cause" the wrath of Yahweh to fall on them like an avenging sword. And yet, particularly in the Book of Job, they also saw the simplism in their own orthodoxy: God also "punishes" the innocent. There is no escaping that fact. And the "answer" to that painful "inequity" is a painful — and humbling — answer: Yahweh is not answerable to us.

Just as each philosophy and religion sees God from its own unique point of view and its own unique place in human history, so too there is not one single and unvarying insight into the nature and personality of Yahweh in the Hebrew Scriptures. Each historian, each poet, each prophet saw Yahweh through his or her own unique personality; there is the effusively romantic poet of the Song of Songs, the gentle Hosea, and the scowly old Jeremiah. And each writer saw Yahweh from his or her own time: peace, war, slavery. Yahweh is not merely the stereotyped

Old Man on the throne, threatening vengeance — a picture most of us tend to see when we think of the Old Testament God. That picture owes more to our memories of Olympian Zeus — and to Charlton Heston smashing the Ten Commandments — than it does to a study of the full Hebrew experience of Yahweh.

There is, to be sure, God the Growler. Given the early anthropomorphism of Hebrew thought, it's hard not to think that Yahweh would get at least a touch put out when Israel consistently missed the whole point of its mission. So you do find, here and there in the Old Testament, Yahweh threatening to come down hard on his rebellious people — and following through on the threat. One point to be made is that that follow-through is historically true: Whenever the people fell into luxury and excess and began running after pagan gods, their very softness and self-indulgence attracted invaders. After awhile, the pattern became obvious, and it needed no special gift of prophetic insight to see that the one state invariably followed the other. What's more, my hunch is that the picture of God the Growler had quite a bit to do with the individual writer's own foul temper, after a lifetime of trying to act as Yahweh's spokesman and being ignored.

Nor, even at his angriest, is Yahweh some kind of Mafia boss whose anger can be assuaged by so many little bribes and blood sacrifices. Psalm 50 says, "Do I eat the flesh of bulls and drink goats' blood?" Unlike the pagan gods, Yahweh does not require placating. God has no needs, only the desire that we fulfill the promise of our Covenant. It is more consistent with Yahweh's character to forgive than to punish.

Most consistent — and probably most basic — is the image of Yahweh the Faithful One. At the innermost core of Judaism there is a single event: the Covenant of Sinai. That event was the beginning of Israel as a religious myth, as a people, and ultimately as a nation. It was a *marriage* between Yahweh and Israel: "I will be your God, and you will be my people." That Covenant was a pledge of faith, and in the centuries that followed — no matter how faithless the people were, Yahweh never lost faith. In complete contrast to the prevailing belief that the God of the Old Testament was unrelievedly angry and unforgiving, we have constant evidence that Yahweh simply refused to give up on them.

Above all, Yahweh is relentlessly *loyal* — even embarrassingly so. In Hosea, Yahweh is pictured as a faithful husband married to a whore, Israel. But rather than abandon her to her lovers, he stands outside the whorehouse door and calls to her. In Zechariah, Yahweh says: "I will whistle to them, gather them in; they will be as numerous as they used to be."

Contrary to the expectations of Scientism, which berates a supposed God for the inefficiency of an evolution that took so long and had so many false starts and dead-ends, the Yahweh of the Old Testament is most definitely *inefficient.* Had efficiency been as high on Yahweh's list of priorities as it is on, say, Carl Sagan's, God never would have given human beings freedom in the first place! God would have made us fully evolved from the start, rather than allowing us freely to achieve our own fulfillment — or not. No, the Yahweh of the Old Testament is most definitely the same inefficient Mind Behind It All whom we discover in the record of evolution. The experience of Israel shows that fulfillment of Yahweh's plan materializes only by fits and starts, progress and regression, two steps backward for every three steps forward. Unlike ourselves, Yahweh must be content with that, since he surely could have made us otherwise.

Another view of Yahweh's personality, perfectly consistent with each of the ones we've seen, is Yahweh the Champion of the Outcasts. If you were to copy out only the passages in the Old Testament in which Yahweh enjoins the people to care for the poor, the widows, the orphans, the strangers, they would fill a small book. Take one such statement, from Exodus: "You must not molest the stranger or oppress him, for *you* lived as strangers in the land of Egypt. You must not be harsh with the widow, or with the orphan. If you are harsh with them, they will cry out to me. And be sure of it: I shall hear their cry. My anger will flare up, and I shall kill you with the sword. And *your* wives will be widows; *your* children will be orphans."

The community of Israel was a *religious* community long before it was a nation. Their Covenant with Yahweh and their Covenant with one another *as* Yahweh's people was the key to their union, not their similar sympathies or their similar bloodlines. Whenever that basic grasp on the Covenant got lost, whenever their individual or tribal differences became more important than their union with Yahweh and with one another as a people, then no leader, no king or prophet, no matter how powerful, could even get a hearing. At such times, they became nothing more than a reluctant "common front," like an uneasy coalition government.

Judaism and Jesus

Not only does Judaism give us profound insights into the nature of God and into human nature in relationship to God, as do the other philosophies and religions we have seen, but it is also impossible really to understand Jesus — and Christianity — without some understanding of Judaism. Jesus was a son of Israel, just as I am a son of my father. Even though I have a quite different personality from my father's, you can still get a better insight into me from knowing something about my father's ethnic background, political leanings, and religious and moral convictions. So too with Jesus and the myth out of which he came.

Reading the gospels and trying to fathom Jesus' meaning without any knowledge of the Old Testament is like trying to read Shakespeare without any knowledge of mythology. Oh, you can "get through it" with some understanding, but a great deal is lost because the symbols and allusions are from a culture much different from our own. Living in cities, we have little "feel" for the objects and situations that Jesus used to explain his message to a simple peasant folk, living off the land — simply because those objects and situations were at the heart of the lives of the people he was trying to explain it to. What do we know of sheep and fish, anointing heads and feet, kings who throw banquets? When Jesus washed his disciples' feet, that was a profoundly moving act, because such things were done by slaves. And he told them — and us — we must wash one another's feet. But today, when a priest or bishop washes twelve peoples' feet on Holy Thursday, it doesn't have the same effect or meaning. For us, in the pews watching, it is almost embarrassing.

What's more, Jesus' audiences often had a quite different understanding of words than we do, hearing them in English. For them, some words had a different "color" or "twist" from our understanding of those same words. (It at least seems that some fundamentalists forget Jesus didn't even speak in English! His words have come down to us from Greek, which was in turn a translation of Jesus' original Aramaic.) It is a cliche that "something gets lost in the translation." A thorough understanding of a foreign speaker's original intention depends in large part not only on the skill of the translator, but on the capacity of the new language to capture the "flavor" of the word from the original language. *Mediocritas,* in Latin, for instance, means simply "average." But that word is highly uncomplimentary when translated into the English "mediocre."

Let one pair of parallel examples of such words suffice for the moment: "perfect" and "holy" — which certainly seem to be a large part of Jesus' message. An English-speaker's understanding of "Be perfect as your heavenly Father is perfect" is that the injunction calls on us to be flawless. But he couldn't have meant that at all, simply because Jesus never asked for the impossible and because his Father *created* us demonstrably imperfect. Only God can be perfect, and if Jesus had demanded that we be perfect, he would have been demanding that we be God —

which is not only impossible but blasphemous. What a Jew meant by "perfect" and "holy" was "whole": all-together, with your "head and heart in the right place," knowing who God is and who you are and which direction you're headed. A Jew knew that we would never "arrive." We are on a journey, and, in the going, we're already there.

Jesus relied on the Old Testament for the only theological language available to his listeners. He spoke as the New Moses; he chose twelve men as representatives of the New Twelve Tribes of the New Israel; he instituted the Eucharist as a New Passover meal to celebrate the liberation from death, just as the first Passover had celebrated Israel's liberation from Egypt. To understand Jesus, you have to have some idea of what Moses, and the Twelve Tribes, and Passover meant to a Hebrew.

Jesus' whole life was lived within Judaism. His preaching presupposed an understanding and acceptance of the Yahweh of whom he was the literal embodiment and of the Covenant between Yahweh and his people. It is hard for the beginner to understand Jesus' reverence for the Hebrew tradition: the Torah. It permeated his whole life and all he was. For him, Israel had always been God's pledge to all humankind to overcome the world and restore all humankind to Paradise: a completely new order. Yet in the texts of the gospels, that motivation in Jesus is all presumed — like the "sub-text" in a play script. Only some understanding of what "made" a Jew can tell a reader what "made" Jesus who he was.

The core of Jesus' message was that the promise of Israel had come true! In him! Again and again, Yahweh had sent improbable heroes to lead them out and begin anew — Adam, Noah, Abraham, Moses. Now, Yahweh had sent the final Hero — the Messiah, the perfectly evolved human being Yahweh had intended from the first. True to character, Yahweh sent an improbable hero — a poor carpenter, from a no-name village, in a no-name province of the Roman Empire. Even more improbably, the Hero won the New Israel not by an act of power, but by an act of abasement; he brought life out from the jaws of death.

There is one trait of the Hebrew People that has underlain all that the chapter has said. Unlike Greek philosophers, Jews were not content to know about God. They wanted to know *God*, person-to-Person.

Now was their chance.

~ Questions for Discussion ~

1. If history can be validly read as a homily, what is God trying to say to us through the events of *our* time? If a prophet or prophetess were to arise today, with a true reading of the mind of Yahweh — angry, loyal, champion of outcasts — what would he or she point to in the world, and especially in America? What items would be on God's priority list of our excesses, our unexamined convictions, our misreading of the world and ourselves? And — in each area — what would he or she call for, to keep us from facing the inevitable effects of our self-induced blindnesses?

2. If such a prophet or prophetess arose and turned his or her attention to the Catholic Church, what would be on the list of priorities? Where is it possible that the Church — not only her leadership but her members — is not genuinely facing the truth about herself and her relationship with the world?

3. To focus the exercise even more tightly: what would a prophet or prophetess with the mind of Yahweh say about your parish or school — its policies and people? Again, not just the administration, but the ordinary folk as well: how they deal with one another, how they honor their "covenant," how they treat "the widows, orphans, strangers": the needy, the nothings, the nerds?

Chapter 6

The Christian Myth

NO SCHOLAR — no matter what religious affiliation or lack of it — would deny that Jesus of Nazareth ever lived. We have testimony even from pagans living around his own time that a holy man from Nazareth, named Jesus, roamed the countryside of Palestine preaching and gathering followers, that he was crucified, and that his followers later claimed that he had risen from the dead.

That much is beyond question. Questions do arise, however, before one even considers the validity of Jesus' message as a personal lifeview that one might adopt: (a) How much of what we read in the gospel is more or less what Jesus really said and intended? (b) Did this Jesus really believe he was the incarnation of God, or was that just an idea dreamed up after his death by his followers? (c) Most crucial of all, according to St. Paul: did Jesus actually rise from the dead? Only after addressing these questions can one appraise Jesus' message in any other than a surface way.

A reader doesn't have to ask those questions about Buddha's message, or Plato's message, or Shakespeare's message, or Karl Marx's message. Granted a little background material about the author may round out the picture a bit, but in the case of those commentators on the human condition, the message stands or falls on its own. The insights are not hindered or helped by knowing that their author was rich or poor, black or white, drunk or sober. *Macbeth* and *Romeo and Juliet* give us insights into ambition and young love, whether they were authored by the same man or each by a committee. Plato's dialogues give insight into human life whether his spokesman, Socrates, ever really lived or was just a literary gimmick.

But the ideas contained in the message of Jesus are not just gentle hints on how to be a nice, generous person and get along well with everybody. The ideas contained in the message of Jesus are volcanic, even though they may seem trite to born Christians. They claim that death, which seems irreversibly real and final, is only real and final from our limited point of view; on the contrary, from God's point of view — which is the truth — death is only apparent and transitional; Jesus claims that we will survive death in a new life. That claim, in turn, rests squarely on the claim that Jesus *is* the Son of God, existent since before any creature was created, equal in nature and status with Yahweh.

And that claim in its turn rests squarely on the testimony of his followers: that Jesus himself was incontestably dead and then was incontestably alive again.

Any reader can study and assess the message of Jesus in exactly the same way as he or she studies and assesses the messages of Buddha, Plato, Shakespeare, and Karl Marx — as if Jesus were "simply another moral philosopher," trying to answer the three basic questions of human suffering. Only one trouble with that: Jesus didn't allow that option. At the very core of Jesus' message is the astonishing claim that he is God, and that union with him will give us a real participation in the life of God — here and hereafter. If that core is not true, then all the rest of the message, no matter how uplifting, is tainted by the fact that Jesus was either a deranged religious fanatic who actually *thought* he was God, or he was a manipulative liar.

If those two claims about Jesus' resurrection and divinity are not true, Jesus and his followers were no better than either lunatics proclaiming they are Napoleon and his generals, or snake-oil salesmen out to milk the suckers.

The Authenticity of the Gospels

Jesus never wrote a book but relied solely on word-of-mouth preaching. Nor are there any reports about the content of his preaching from a non-Christian source. (Anyone who found Jesus' message worth the trouble of recording had already been convinced and converted.) Therefore, we see Jesus only through the members of early Christian communities. How did their current interests, years after Jesus' death, affect their passing-on of the tradition? How much did they "put on Jesus' lips," having Jesus answer problems that were not problems during his lifetime but became problems after his death?

One point in favor of the gospels' accuracy is that, if the authors had been a self-serving group, they surely didn't censor out what the audience would find too tough to take: "If you want to find your true self, you have to forget yourself; it's as easy for a rich man to get into the Kingdom as for a camel to pass through the eye of a needle; get rid of your grudge before you make your offering." Not to mention the divinity of Jesus and his resurrection.

Most glaring of all: surely they would have left out — or tamed down — the crucifixion, unless they had anchored themselves to the historical truth. Crucifixion was the most degrading of Roman capital punishments, reserved only for rebels, runaway slaves, and enemies of the people. In opting to include the crucifixion, the early Church was committing itself to defend a myth system that was *validated* by a *failure!* A smart PR person would have cut a great deal of that kind of stuff out of the gospels.

Moreover, the authors of the gospels took no pains to "cover-up" the obvious and continuous mess-ups on the part of the men who were the very heroes of their stories. The Twelve almost invariably miss Jesus' point; their motives all along seem to be embarrassingly materialistic: finding out who gets the most power when they inherit this "Kingdom." The very *last* question they ask, just at the moment of the Ascension — after the excruciating experience of the crucifixion and the exhilarating experience of the resurrection — is: "Are you going to restore the Kingdom *now?*"

The authors don't balk at showing the disciples as craven cowards, who hiked up their skirts and ran at the first sign of any real opposition. One of them betrayed Jesus to the authorities. Another — the man who became head of the Church — is shown quite clearly by the gospels as a braggart, a coward, and a liar, who denied even knowing Jesus, not once, but three times, with plenty of time between to realize what he had done — and not to a guard with a spear at his throat, but to a waitress!

Further, the gospels seem quite subdued in comparison to the style of other Near Eastern mystery cults of the time. They are not the raving of ecstatics, but sober and calm. Matthew is at times given to some excess, but that can be written off as Spielberg "special effects," which have little effect on the main message and which clarified it in the minds of Matthew's primarily Jewish audience by allusion to Hebrew Scripture. Also, the characters in the gospel are not cartoon figures — the starched heroes and snarling villains you find in works like *Beowulf* or the Viking sagas. They are just ordinary "folks," with virtues and shortcomings. They "ring true."

Also, biblical scholars have probed through the layers of the language, input of successive editors, and questions raised in the New Testament (like archaeologists at a dig) to a level that is undoubtedly the words and concerns of a single, consistent, Aramaic mind. Some of what the gospels say may be the authors' putting words on Jesus' lips, having him solve problems of which a man of his time would not have been aware, but all of those additions seem consistent with the message of that single Aramaic mind at their root. (For an exhaustive study of this question consult a book like the *Jerome Biblical Commentary*.)

Could the gospels have been the product of the "collective mind" of the disappointed Apostles? Highly doubtful, considering the men one finds in the gospels themselves! Surely such men would have "papered over" their own obvious stupidity. They could have gotten away with it (Homer did; Virgil did).

What's more, anyone who has tried to formulate a new philosophy with a committee will tell you it just can't be done. To create such an *organic* system of insights, each one so consistent with the others and with the whole, would take the work of a single mind — and a genius at that.

One final aspect to this first question: The gospels did not begin to be written until a generation after Jesus' death, and each by a person or group who did not have direct contact with Jesus (despite legends that Mark was the man who ran away naked at Jesus' arrest and that the author of "John" was the one who leaned his head against Jesus' chest at the Last Supper).

None of the gospels even claims to be the gospel of Jesus Christ; only "the gospel of Jesus Christ *according* to Matthew," etc. Each has his own easily discernible personality: Mark the breathless amateur, Matthew the fire-breathing lawyer, Luke the gentle, John the rhapsodic theologian. Each has his personal vision of the Christian myth, and his own personal axes to grind.

How could those later authors be sure of the authenticity of their work? How could they be sure their personal viewpoints didn't skew what they were documenting?

To that question I can give only an analogy: The authors of the gospels did exactly what any anchor person does in a studio in New York or L.A., when a story comes in from reliable reporters in Beirut or Johannesburg. I began to understand that process for the first time when I was asked to write a book that eventually was published as *The Voice of Blood.* Five Jesuits had been murdered: in El Salvador, Brazil, and Zimbabwe. I had never been in any of those places. I had never met — nor even heard of — the five men. So, I plowed through *National Geographic,* through reports in English, Spanish, and Portuguese papers. I wrote Jesuits in the three countries asking for anything they might know about those men and their assassinations.

Gradually, I built up a file of notes, photocopies, and tapes sent from men on the spot when the murders had taken place. So, I wrote. When I had "finished," I sent what I had written to my correspondents for their critique. Then, with their corrections in hand, I went back for a rewrite. When the book was published, it was as authentic as anyone could expect it to be.

I can just see whoever "Mark" or "Luke" was, down at the docks in Ostia when a new shipload of Jews came, in flight from the Roman destruction of Jerusalem: "Hey, you got any good Jesus stories?" And then, checking the final drafts out with men and women who had been actual eyewitnesses, just in case.

It is very difficult to imagine writers laboring as hard as I do to write, trying to "sell" a manuscript about justice, generosity, and selflessness — and yet themselves working from a motive of deception, self-interest, and materialism. There are, to be sure, ministers of religion who have used religion as no more than a commodity to be sold, like laundry detergent or life insurance. But what profit did the gospel writers reap from their "deception"? Death.

Was Jesus God?

The gospels quote Jesus claiming divinity, explicitly: "I and the Father are one." Whatever else he was, Jesus was a Jew, a member of a community whose greatest contact point with God in all their history was Moses. And yet at what scholars agree is the most "un-retouched" level of the gospels, Jesus is not just another rabbi interpreting Moses. He is, in fact, *correcting* Moses: "You have heard it said... but *I* tell you...." There is no parallel to Jesus' claims in any other Hebrew prophet. To declare himself capable of changing the Law of Moses made him either a lunatic, or a con man... or the Messiah.

His followers were convinced he was God — not *a* god, but the embodiment of Yahweh himself. To think that a Jew — and all the Apostles were Jews — was capable of *conceiving* such an idea was preposterous. There was *one* God; no more profound, basic truth to a Jew's belief. Yet these Jews did believe Jesus was God, and gave testimony to that belief with their lives — and deaths.

Even if the miracles of Jesus could ever be "proven" to be exaggerations or later additions, even if the early Church could have had Jesus "solving" problems that were not problems in his time, there is one unarguable piece of evidence that Jesus at least *claimed* to be God: the indictment for his execution. To give his executioners credit, they did not execute Jesus because he was simply one more "moral philosopher." At his trial before the Jewish elders, there is only one question on the docket: "Are you the Christ, the son of the Holy One?" He is on trial precisely for his claim that he is the Son of God. And Jesus answers (in Mark), "I am" — words no pious Jew would dare speak, because they are the true name of Yahweh.

Jesus' claims were *so* outrageous that the whole Jewish mob, which had cheered him through the streets a week earlier, turned completely against him and screamed for his death. So outrageous that his claims created an unprecedented coalition between the Pharisees and the Sadducees — who never before had joined sides on *any* question. Jesus was not just another dissident.

Jesus was, in fact, giving the Jews an utterly new face of God, one they had never seen before: not the Legalist, but the Father. What's more, he laid claim to this new insight not by invoking inspiration from divine authority (as Moses and the prophets had), but by evoking divine *equality* . It is the only explanation for the dramatic change in the people and in the natural enemies among the Jewish leadership, the only reason Jesus was executed and others were not. It might also explain why even his friend Judas really turned against him.

There is no doubt that Jesus claimed divinity. He either was what he claimed, or a lunatic, or a liar.

But the rest of Jesus' message does not seem to be the message of a lunatic or a liar. In his entire life, all he did was heal — bodies with his hands and souls with his words. There is nothing fanatic in his actions, and there is nothing underhanded in his doctrine; quite the contrary: It speaks of nothing but open-handedness and open-heartedness, which he himself not only constantly preached but consistently practiced. He made no money; he didn't even have a home. And — most persuasive of all — as his disciples did, he went to his death when denying his claim would have saved his life.

There is one related question that gives some readers of the gospels difficulty: if Jesus knew he was God, then it was "easy" for him; he knew it was going to turn out all right. And yet, how could he have undergone such gut-wrenching doubt in the Garden on the night before his arrest? Why was the second-last thing he said, "My God, my God, why have you abandoned me?" If he knew he was God, he would surely have known God had not betrayed him. Was he merely quoting a psalm? Was he simply "faking" it?

St. Paul answers the question of Jesus' consciousness of his divinity, at least to my satisfaction, in Philippians: "He had always the nature of God, yet he did not cling to his equality with God, but instead he *emptied* himself, to assume the state of a slave and became as all human beings are."

Jesus did not un-God himself at the incarnation. He couldn't cease to be what he was. Instead, he freely became "amnesiac" about his true nature, and he was born and, as the gospels say, "he grew in wisdom and in age and in grace." He learned, just as we do. But it would be utterly impossible for anyone to "learn" if he had at the same time the full possession of the knowledge of God. Instead, Jesus "emptied himself." He discovered who he was, just as we do. And he doubted his convictions about himself and his mission, just as we do.

At his baptism at John's hands, he had the thunderous realization: "You are my Son." Immediately thereafter, he went out in the wilderness to cope with that realization, and he was tempted — on *precisely* that conviction: "If you *are* the Son of God, turn these stones into bread." Then he emerged from the wilderness and went to the synagogue. And in front of the people, he read from the scroll of Isaiah: "The spirit of the Lord has been given to me, for he has anointed me." In the garden and on the cross, Jesus endured true, soul-searing doubt. But his last words were an act of faith: "Father, into your hands I commend my spirit." Christianity is the only myth of human meaning I know of whose God endured doubt. Like me. Like you.

The Resurrection

The gospels record no witnesses at the actual resurrection, at the moment when the stone rolled back and Jesus came forth alive again. It would have been a simple matter to "stage" a real audience-grabber: thunder, rocks cracking, and Jesus steps forward in a blaze of light! But they didn't. We have only the word of the many people who claim to have seen Jesus alive again. How can they be trusted? The only substantial answer to that question is the one given before: They went to their deaths, when denial of their claim would have set them free.

At the time of Jesus' execution, the gospels declare — very forthrightly — his disciples panicked. They fled to the room of the Last Supper and locked themselves in. They were, in a word, cowards. At that shattering moment of Jesus' defeat, the Church had — to all intents and purposes — ceased to exist. Yet, fifty days later, on Pentecost, they came out ablaze with courage! A courage unto death. It's hard, at least for me, to witness so many people manifest such courage, for so long, and even into death — for a hoax? Like their Master, they received no profit from their preaching, only persecution and death.

Something earth-shattering must have occurred to account for such a radical conversion from craven cowards to unflinching Apostles. They claim that experience was encountering the risen Jesus. And for every one of them, their testimony was a "death-bed confession." I, at least, have to accept their word.

Add to all that the growth of the Christian community since that time, from a handful of fishermen and peasants to a worldwide body of believers. It is miraculous that any merely human organization could last so long, withstanding not only attacks from without but also outlasting its own enormous stupidities attacking them from within: the early battles over the true nature of Jesus, schisms, the Crusades, the Inquisition — to name only a few of many. The magnitude of the spiritual change this Mustard Seed effected, the profound way in which it changed history, so suddenly and yet so permanently, simply can't be explained by the ardor of a few disciples. There is only one source adequate to that effect: the personality of Jesus.

The Personality of Jesus

Quite often, unfairly, the *image* you have of people often adversely affects your acceptance of them. If someone's appearance "puts you off," it's likely you won't really spend too much time trying to get to know that person or to listen too carefully to what that person says. This is just as true of Jesus as of anyone else.

Most people's image of Jesus — the way he looked — is based on religious art, holy pictures, and biblical movies, which, almost without exception, picture him as white, blue-eyed, pale, delicate, and most definitely otherworldly. Such pictures do not show that Jesus was clearly male, much less human. If that is your image of him, then you quite likely won't spend much time getting to know him or listening too carefully to what he says.

Of course all such religious art is a lie. Well-intentioned, perhaps (to make us good, gentle boys and girls), but still a lie. Jesus couldn't have looked like that. He was a Jew; swarthy skin, dark eyes, out in the blistering sun all day. Look at a carpenter's body sometime, especially his hands. Jesus was flogged with leaded whips, battered around, booted through the streets, stretched out with his raw back in the dirt and nailed to the beam of a cross. And he lasted three hours! Hard to see the holy-card Jesus enduring all that.

Such well-intentioned — but nonetheless untrue — religious art emphasizes only the "feminine" side of Jesus, which was truly there, as it should be in all well-rounded males: kindness, gentleness, sensitivity, approachability — especially to the needy and to children. But there is another whole side to Jesus that is in the gospels but that doesn't get into much church art or biblical movies (or hymns) — his "masculine" side: aggressiveness, authority, decisiveness, confidence.

The "gentle Jesus art" fails to remember Jesus stood up in public, before the Jewish elders and their spies, and changed the laws of Moses: "The sabbath was made for people, not people for the sabbath." He called those same elders rather uncomplimentary names: "snakes, whitewashed tombs, blind guides fit for hell" — among others. He had an inordinate dislike for hypocrisy, especially among the well-placed, and never missed a chance to point it out. He cleaned the money changers from the Temple with only a handful of rope and his own moral indignation. He most definitely did not always turn the other cheek himself, not when there was need for rage.

Jesus must have been a powerful presence; only that would explain the triumphant "Hosannahs" of Palm Sunday. But what can explain the profound effect that personality has had on the hearts and minds of billions who never met him, the cathedrals, hospitals, and universities erected in his name, the incredible effect his myth has had on two thousand years of human history?

The Message of Jesus

All the myths we have seen are trying to answer the same question: What are we here for? What must I do to live the only life I have to the fullest? Jesus answered that question, too. In fact, Jesus *is* the answer to that question. "I am the way." Not "I am the path," as in, "Like a bridge over troubled waters, I will lay me down" — and all we have to do is walk over Jesus into security. No, "I'm the way it's done. If you want to live your one life to the fullest, be like me."

What Jesus is saying is: "You set your sights too low." You were not made to be a secure loner, isolated or insulated from the world. You were not made in such a way that you can be fulfilled by money, fame, sex, and power. You were not made for absorption into the All. You were not made to strain for unrealizable perfection. You were made to be, as Jesus was, the fully evolved human being. Creation has evolved from inanimate matter, to vegetative life, to animal life, to human life, and now it is ready for the ultimate step: to divine life. You are called by God to share in the sonship of Jesus, to share the aliveness of God — now and forever.

There is the mystery that separates Christianity from all other myths, philosophies, religions. The Hebrews came closest to it, realizing we are men and women *sought* by God. But what Jesus offers the Christian is not just a love-covenant but a bonding-together of God and humanity. Jesus no longer has any hands or voice except our hands and voices. Just as Jesus is the bodying-forth of the invisible God, *we,* the Christian Church, are now the bodying-forth of Jesus — his physical presence in the world, animated by his Spirit.

"From the beginning till now, the entire creation, as we know, has been groaning in one great act of giving birth." When St. Paul wrote that, he knew nothing about evolution. But he understood the heart of the message of Jesus.

We are the sons and daughters of God, Peers of the Realm. But *noblesse oblige:* if we are indeed God's sons and daughters, we have to begin *acting* like his sons and daughters: like Jesus.

Acting like Jesus does not mean literally to heal lepers, to cast out demons, to forgive sinners — at least not for most of us. But we can't read the message of the gospel with "materialist eyes," as if the only lepers were physical lepers. There are "lepers" everywhere you turn. They're surely in your neighborhood, office, school: the girl no one ever asks out, the boy who always eats his lunch alone, the widow up the block. They don't walk around ringing bells, but they're lepers. And you can heal them — or at least begin trying. You are a son or daughter of God: *noblesse oblige.*

And there are demons aplenty around you, too: slaves to perfectionism, people obsessed with their looks (good or bad), victims of diabolic self-distaste. And you can heal them — or at least begin trying. You are a son or daughter of God: *noblesse oblige.* And there are people you can forgive, not as a priest forgives, but as a human heart forgives. I'll bet you can think of at least one right now. Then do it. *Noblesse oblige.*

According to Jesus, there is only *one* norm in the eyes of God that will decide whether the one life you had was fulfilled or not. At the Judgment, there is only one question. Not how many times you got your name in the paper, or how much money you made, how many people you had "under" you. Nor how many times did you masturbate or marry or use a condom. Only one question about the worth of your life: "I was hungry; I was thirsty; I was the one they called 'worthless.' What did you do about that?"

A Christian adopts the *attitudes* of Jesus, which are the attitudes of God. It could be summed up in the person of the Father of the Prodigal Son: waiting every night for the boy to return, running eagerly to him, hushing his shame-faced memorized speech, and wrapping his arms around the boy. That is the God of Jesus Christ, the God in whose image you were created to evolve. If I had to sum up the entire gospel in two words, it would be the two words of Jesus from the cross: "Father, forgive."

The God of Jesus Christ forgives instead of condemning, sets free instead of tying down with endless laws, chooses the sinner over the self-righteous, the adulteress over her hypocritical judges. This is a God for whom the commandments exist for the human person, not the other way round, a God who detests the discrimination that sets "us" against "them," a God for whom Jesus is the standard of what being human means.

Noblesse oblige.

The Christian Church

The New Testament was written in Greek, the common language of the Roman Empire. But the Greek word *ekklēsia,* ("assembly, church") is used only twice in all four gospels. And scholars dispute both instances, arguing that the term was inserted later, after "the Church" had become a reality. Far more common in the gospels is the term *basileia tou theou* ("the Kingdom of God"). *Basileia* occurs over a hundred times in the New Testament.

Luke is the author both of the gospel that bears his name and of the Acts of the Apostles. But when Luke writes in his gospel, he uses the word *basileia* ("Kingdom") about forty times for the Christian community, yet in Acts he uses that word only seven times, and instead, now, prefers the word *ekklēsia* ("Church").

Something has happened between Luke's writing his gospel version and Luke's writing Acts. Quite likely it was that the very earliest Church took Jesus *literally;* they thought the "Kingdom," the end of this world and the beginning-over was going to take place *on* this planet — literally and soon: "a new heaven and a new earth." Only one problem: It didn't happen. Back to re-examine again. Then the realization, slowly, as always: not the Kingdom the Apostles expected (a literal new Kingdom of David, in which they'd wear gold robes and have power), nor the end-time Kingdom (a new heaven and a new earth), but a community on the march to fulfillment: a Once-and-Future-Kingdom.

The term *basileia* covers both: the Kingdom on earth, on the march, and the Kingdom in heaven, fulfilled. Our souls, our true inner selves, are in both at once: immanent and transcendent.

But the word *ekklēsia* ("Church") is reserved for the this-world phase of the Kingdom: today's Christian community.

The metaphor that best captures the reality of the this-world Kingdom is the one frequently used by Vatican II: "The Pilgrim Church."
Like Chaucer's travelers to Canterbury, we are on our way to a shrine,
but we haven't yet arrived. (And, oh! Let us hope we can be as merry a
lot as Chaucer's pilgrims!)

Our career as Christians is a journey. Like the Hebrews, we are an
Exodus community. Like Adam, Noah, Abraham, Moses, the Apostles,
we are called from our comfortable ghettoes and neighborhoods and
suburbs. We are even called from our comfortable earth!

We are by no means perfect. We are not "there." And any time we
think we are, we ought to sit down and re-examine! Yet, in the going,
we are already there.

There is little sense of "structure" in the New Testament Christian
community, in the sense of an organized "institution." None whatever
in the gospels themselves; simply the Apostles and other disciples, male
and female, gathered around Jesus. A real community. The binding force
is not a structure of rules and "lines of authority" but the presence and
personality of Jesus.

Even in Paul's letters and the Acts of the Apostles, there seems little external structure — though more than there is in the gospels. In
Acts, we are beginning to deal with a far larger and more differentiated
group, spreading all over the known world, raising problems that weren't
problems Jesus had to face. Peter is "where the buck stops"; James, as
bishop of Jerusalem, also seems to have some kind of "authority," at
least by honor; Paul feels obliged to "check in" with them — and also
feels obliged to tell them when he thinks they are wrong (circumcising
Gentile converts, forcing Gentiles to observe the Jewish dietary laws).

As the numbers of converts increased, there was need for more division of responsibilities: offices. The Twelve could not be the only ones
to celebrate the Eucharist, not when there were communities waiting
for Mass all over the Mediterranean basin. Nor could even the newly
ordained priests and bishops cope with all the needs of the faithful, not
merely their spiritual needs but their physical needs as well. Thus, they
instituted the office of deacon and deaconess, men and women who
could not celebrate the Eucharist, but could at least "spell" the priests
and bishops and deal not only with such matters as caring for the needs
of the sick and aged and destitute, but could also give Communion, accept the vows of married couples, and preach when no ordained priest
was likely to pass through for quite some time. That office lasted for
nearly eleven hundred years, then fell into disuse, but (because of a new
shortage of priests) it has been recently reactivated — at least for males.

The bureaucracy of the Church we know today — even in non-Catholic Christian Churches — was something almost unknown in those early Christian communities. Bishops, priests, deacons and deaconesses, yes; but apparently all with far less sense of "territorial rights" than we know today. However, only a fool would think a worldwide organization could be administered solely on the basis of the good will of the members and "gentle persuasion" on the part of the administrators.

Like dentists, teachers, and the IRS, church administrators may seem to some a mixed blessing, but they are necessary to a worldwide enterprise. There has to be a focus. You can't have a team without a captain or a play without a director.

The first service to the Church Paul mentions is "the gift of preaching with wisdom." "Administration" comes quite a bit further down the list. Remember that the Latin root of "administer" is *ministrare,* "to serve," and at the root of that root is *minis,* "less than." It is for that reason the pope, proudly, refers to himself as "the servant of servants of God."

How the administration of the Church became a hierarchy, the Magisterium, will have to wait for another chapter.

The Gateway to the Kingdom: Metanoia

It is astonishing (to me) how few even churchgoing Christians really grasp what they mean when they claim to be Christians, members of the *basileia tou theou.* "The aliveness of God is in *you,* now!" Yawn. It is to such people — his own disciples — that Jesus groaned so often, "Oh, ye of little faith!" So wedded to surfaces, so blind to inner truths.

The greatest problem one faces with born-Christians is that they have been baptized — but they have never been *converted.*

They go to Mass; they go to religious ed classes; they "pay their dues." But they have never had the gut-wrenching realization Jesus had at the moment of his baptism: God saying, "You are my Son!" Jesus put it perfectly in a metaphor we have all heard hundreds of times, but perhaps never truly heard — not in the way we hear when the dentist says, "You have five cavities."

Jesus said that discovering the Kingdom, the Christian community, was like discovering a treasure in a field. (Yawn.) But think about it. There you are, bopping along in your field, when suddenly your toe hits some object. "La!" you say. "My toe has struck an object. It looks like a box." And you dig away, and, whaddya know! It *is* a box! And you crack open the box. And it's filled with diamonds, and rubies, and gold! And it's all *yours!* I don't know what you'd say at that moment, but, vulgar as I am, I know what I'd say: "Holy [*beep*]!"

So what Jesus is saying is that, if you haven't discovered that you're part of the Kingdom of God, the Christian community, and said, "Holy [*beep*]!" then you *haven't* found the Kingdom of God yet! You may be baptized, but you've never been converted.

The word "conversion" in the gospels doesn't mean changing over to a new Church with a different label, like changing your registration from "Democrat" to "Republican": "I used to be a Jew, but now I'm a Christian." It reaches down into the innermost depths of your soul — your self, your character, your how-I-look-at-things. It's like somebody with severe eye problems suddenly getting his or her first pair of glasses!

"Conversion" is a change so radical that it can be described only in approximate, symbolic terms to someone who's never undergone it. The fiery conversion of Moses on Sinai, the thunderous "conversion" of Jesus at his baptism, the blazing conversion of St. Paul on the road to Damascus. (When my own conversion came, my own "acceptance of being accepted," the only way I could describe it was "like drowning in light," as difficult to describe to someone who's never undergone it as describing the "conversion" of puberty to someone who has not yet undergone it.)

The Greek word used by the authors of the New Testament is *meta-noia* (*meta* = "after" as in "metamorphosis" and *noia* = "way of thinking" as in "paranoia"), which means literally "a total reversal of thinking," a change of mind upon reflection, as in "I was *wrong!*" But that is, alas, not something many of us want to say.

Metanoia is an insight, beyond the surfaces of reality to a level beneath — like my experience with the black Lab, when I suddenly realized that I knew God's mind about as well as the Lab knew mine. That wasn't a major metanoia, not a major "Holy [*beep*]!" But a meaningful and significant one for me. "The real thing," though, is a new realization, at the roots of your being, about what life is all about, a shattering of your horizons, a transformation of what you believe is possible for a human being to achieve: "You have set your sights too low."

The genuine Christian sees that, in order to be human at its *fullest,* we must strive to be like Jesus: the embodiment of God.

Merely "going through the motions" of baptism, confirmation, Mass, is not the gateway into the Christian community. That is no better than the grudging dutifulness of the elder brother of the Prodigal Son. As Jesus himself put it to Nicodemus, conversion is a reversal as radical as returning to your mother's womb and starting all over again.

The disciples came to Jesus and said, "Who is the greatest in the

Kingdom of God?" So he called a little child to him and set the child in front of them. Then he said, "One who makes himself as little as this little child is the greatest in the Kingdom of Heaven."

The only thing between us and the Kingdom is our pseudosophistication, our belief that possessions and looks and power are any indication of our true worth, our dependence on the expectations of others and their ideas of what is "acceptable." All that stands between us and the Light is our own stubborn, self-chosen blindness.

~ Questions for Discussion ~

1. Think for a moment of the "lepers" in your neighborhood, office, class. Now focus down to just one. Get the face. Now, what are you going to do to "heal" that leper — or at least begin trying? *Noblesse oblige.*

2. Most ordinary people don't waste much time scrounging around for arguments to prove that Plato or Shakespeare was a complete hoax. Scholars might, but not most people. Yet quite a few people spend a great deal of time scrounging up arguments against the authenticity of the gospels, the divinity of Jesus, the value of membership in an organized Christian Church. Why?

If they ever admitted Jesus really is the embodiment of God, the privileged expression of God's ideal for us, and that the Church he founded — however many faults it may have in realizing that ideal — is God's will for us, what would they have to do?

Chapter 7

The Seed and the Shoot

A SEED IS A DANDY CREATION. Everything the tree will later be is compacted into that tiny bit. The tree is going to look quite different, and yet is fundamentally the same entity.

But the seed — the gospel of Jesus — is not the tree. It is not a comprehensive textbook of theology, plus a practical book of regulations for any eventuality, plus a scrupulously plotted map showing where the Christian Community is going. The gospel is a call to metanoia, to a whole reversal of the world's values. After that, we're on our own to face whatever comes.

The gospel message doesn't foresee what was then unforeseeable. Jesus said nothing about a hierarchical Church. He put Peter in charge and let the community face that when they came to it; that's what his Father had given them brains for. Jesus never compared his relationship to the community with the relationship of a head to a body. He left that to Paul.

I said before that, if Jesus came back for an inspection tour, he'd almost surely have some suggestions. But he had to realize the tree would look *different* from the seed. Being "rooted in the gospel" doesn't mean being locked back inside the mustard seed. There are still dreamers who yearn for the Church of the first century — as the Anabaptists did in the sixteenth century. That would be like destroying all motor vehicles because of air pollution and going back to ox-drawn carts.

The "original design" of the first communities is normative in their *spirit*, but not in their custom and practice. As we have seen several times, all myth systems physicalize their beliefs in symbolic writings, objects, places, and activities. Some of those symbols are essential. Eucharist, for instance, is an essential of the Christian myth; the language it's celebrated in is not. We have to separate what is essential from the merely culturally conditioned, that is, separate those basic insights from the ways those insights were concretized into symbols, customs, and practices to make them meaningful to a people of a particular time and culture.

74

Thus, bread and wine as the elements of the Eucharist are quite likely an essential, not only because Jesus used them, but because they physicalize a truth — bread for nourishment and wine for joy — which is transcultural; they mean the same thing in all cultures. On the other hand, circumcising male adults as an initiation rite into the Kingdom had meaning only in the Hebrew culture and it could (mercifully) be considered not essential.

Thus, whatever follows in these next four chapters on the apostolic Church and the Church of the next nineteen centuries is not merely a jolly jaunt through history to provide "exam fodder," but it is an attempt to distil out what is essential in any authentic Christian community and what is merely a passing phase (even if the "phase" lasted a few hundred years).

The standard by which one separates the essential from the changeable is the person of Jesus: the elements in the Church he would recognize as authentic developments, and the elements that are all right for one phase and not for another, as well as the elements that violate completely what Jesus intended. Although the gospels never quote Jesus condemning slavery, anti-Semitism, or nuclear war, it is difficult not to assume he would. On the other hand, it is difficult to imagine him giving his blessing to the Inquisition, the Renaissance popes, or the Crusades.

The tree must be fundamentally the same as the seed. If you plant a peach pit, you don't expect to get burrs — or even good apples. The tree may have good years and bad years; it may grow suckers that have to be pruned away. But if it turns into something other than a peach tree, it's lost contact with its origins. The body of the Church may be different from the body of the first communities — as the body of an adult is different from what it was as a fetus. But the heart and soul must be the same — matured, of course, but still the same.

If the essence of the Church has changed, not the metaphors we use to explain it, nor external changes to respond to new times and peoples, but its *essence*, then we do not have the Church of Christ. We have merely a succession of "churches," each overpowering and taking the place of the previous one, like the barbarian invaders of Roman Europe.

We should not fall victim to the simplism that wants us to reproduce the early communities literally. But neither should we fall victim to the opposite simplism: that the Christian Church has changed so radically over the centuries that the first community has nothing left to tell us. Whatever our adaptations to unexpected challenges, if we continue to be "Christian," we have to be consistent with the intentions of our Founder, which were best known by the community he founded — not rationally and explicitly, but intuitively and surely, as friends would know what their Friend would do in a situation he had not foreseen.

How do we avoid "putting onto the lips of Jesus" insights of which he would disapprove? Fr. Raymond Brown has good advice:

> A good practical rule for avoiding self-deception is to pay more attention to scripture when it *disagrees* with what we want to hear than when it agrees. When the Bible disagrees with the spirit of our times, it is not always because the biblical authors are giving voice to a limited, out-of-date religious view. Frequently, it is because God's ways are not ours.

The Church of Peter and Paul (ca. 30–65)

The Christian communities we find in Acts may not have been as idealized as Luke makes them seem:

> The faithful all lived together and owned everything in common. They sold their goods and possessions and shared out the proceeds among themselves according to what each one needed. . . . No one was ever in want, as all those who owned houses sold them and brought the money to the apostles. Then it was distributed to any members who might be in need. (Acts 2:44-45, 4:34–35)

It is clear such "communism" was not the norm of belonging to the community, judging from what Paul says to and about other communities in his letters. Nonetheless, overall, the communities were remarkably generous to one another, even to foreign communities whose members the supporting community had never met. So generous were they that Paul had to caution them that they needn't impoverish themselves to help others. A similar situation exists today when a wealthy suburban parish will offer to support a poor inner-city parish, or a diocese will do the same for a diocese in a Third World country.

The earliest communities lived in exactly the same milieu Jesus had lived in a few years before and continued the Jewish customs they had known since childhood. They met in the Temple and synagogues, paid the Temple tax, and — surprisingly — submitted in some degree to the judgment of the Temple, despite Jesus' critical attitude toward its leaders and his consistent demand for religious freedom from the Pharisees' strictures. The disciples answered charges before the same council that had condemned Jesus. In defending their beliefs they began to probe them more deeply themselves and discovered supporting texts in the Hebrew Scriptures — all of which influenced the writing of the gospels.

One member of the elders, a rabbi named Gamaliel, proposed a test for this new "sect" that is as valid today as two thousand years ago: If this new movement is of God, why worry about it? If it is of God, it will continue no matter what we do. And so it has.

But gradually the disciples' preaching pushed the elders too far, and they were forbidden to preach — which, of course, men and women with such a mission simply couldn't abide by. Persecutions began, led by a zealous young Greek-speaking, ultra-conservative Pharisee named Saul. Unlikely as it was (to anyone not used to the way God chooses heroes), this Saul was to become the first great theologian of the very Church he was hunting down.

But dissension also seethed within the Church (which has continued to this day). Already, within the few years since Jesus' death, despite the somewhat rosy picture in Acts, bickering began between Greek-speaking Jewish Christians and Hebrew-speaking Jewish Christians over distribution of funds. Thus the institution of the diaconate, to see that no one was left unserved.

Part of the need to spread administration was that the Apostles were on the move — and on the run. Persecution proved providential, since it sent the Apostles outside the tight confines of Jerusalem. And the persecution also brought Saul.

As Saul was walking the road to Damascus to hunt out more of the Christian "heretics" from Judaism, suddenly, beyond the words to express it, Saul encountered God. It was like an incredible light that struck him down. "Saul, Saul, why are you persecuting me?" And Saul remembered asking, "Who are you, Lord?" And the voice answered, "I am Jesus of Nazareth; you are persecuting me."

Paul does not say he was converted by the historical, flesh-and-blood Jesus, as the other Apostles were. He says he encountered "the risen Lord." Therefore, before the gospels were written, we have written proof that the earliest Christians believed Jesus had risen from the dead.

People would feel more comfortable if they had testimony of the risen Jesus from a neutral observer. But we have! And not just a neutral observer, but from a dedicated Christian-basher!

The Council of Jerusalem

The gospel spread out of Jerusalem, and then beyond Palestine to Jewish enclaves scattered all over the known world (the Diaspora), then even outside the Jewish ghettoes to interested — uncircumcised — pagans.

Thus the first major conflict of doctrine in the new Church and its first "council" to decide the issue.

Potential converts wanted to become Christians, and Paul and other missionaries obliged — without requiring that the males be circumcised. In the central community, Peter himself had accepted Gentile converts, but the community, hemmed around by threats from orthodox Jews, insisted on circumcision, to show the elders that Christians were not heretical Jews but only a new sect of Judaism that claimed the Messiah had come.

This critical event is important for understanding the nature of Christ's Church. On the one hand, the opinion of the Twelve with Peter at their head was normative; they were in the best position to judge what Jesus himself would have done had he been presented with this new problem. On the other hand, any group of Christians could and did nonetheless present its case against the position taken by the mother community because, as Paul insisted, of "the liberty we enjoy in Christ Jesus."

In the early Church, as in any large organization, there were widely different points of view on what the real nature of the Church and her mission were. On the Right, the conservatives, many of them converted Pharisees (and, according to Paul, some infiltrators) wanted to remain, in effect, a sect of Judaism; on the Left, the liberals, Paul and those on the mission to emigré Jews and to the Gentiles, believed it was Jesus' clear intention to leave behind — entirely — both the restrictive Law and the Temple. At the Center were Peter, James, and others, who seem to have been leaning first to one side, then to the other.

Part of this can be explained by something we have seen before: the difference between the Hebrew mind and Greek mind, not just a difference in language, but in the ways of *thinking*. The Hebrew was more right-brain, the Greek (even Jews, like Paul, brought up among Greeks) more left-brain. Hebrews were loyal to a culture; Greeks more open to new ideas. The Hebrews feared contamination; Greeks feared missing out on a truth that was right in front of their noses but unexplored.

But there was more. The Jewish Church, mostly conservative, knew from experience that, if they were careful and accommodating, the Temple would tolerate them, as it did other dissident sects, as it would have tolerated Jesus if he hadn't gone as far as blasphemy. There was a narrow line between being a separate Jewish sect and being reabsorbed back into Judaism, but the Right was willing to walk it.

Paul was a formidable force. The blazing insight of his conversion left no room for pussy-footing. As the great Protestant missionary Albert Schweitzer said, Paul is "the patron saint of thought in Christianity. ... All those who plan to serve the gospel of Christ by destroying the liberty of thinking must hide their faces from him."

In the New Testament, there are two descriptions of the Council of Jerusalem, which met to handle the question of how to deal with the Gentiles: Must they, in effect, become Jews before they could become Christians? One version is in Paul's letter to the Galatians, and one in Luke's Acts of the Apostles. But Paul was an eyewitness to the council, and Luke was not, writing nearly thirty years later. In Luke, there was a fierce debate, solved by compromise: the Gentiles need not be circumcised, but they should follow some of the Jewish rules about diet.

Paul's version in Galatians says: "I opposed Peter to his face, because he was so obviously wrong!" There was a far deeper question on the table at this Council (and afterward) than merely circumcision of male Gentiles or what foods they could "legitimately" eat. As Paul says, the Hebrew-speaking (and *thinking*) Church in Jerusalem "wants to reduce us all to slavery" to the Hebrew Law. At the profoundest level, the real question before the Council was whether Jesus had founded a new religion, and, beneath that, was Jesus merely a good man who founded a Jewish sect, or was Jesus God, with far greater power than Moses?

Paul explained his case, and there was a lengthy discussion. At the end, Peter announced the decision of the community: One is saved not by the Law, nor by circumcision, but by the grace of Jesus Christ. The highest authority of Christianity had changed its mind: Something they had thought was essential was not.

They divided up their mission: "agreeing that we [Paul and his people] would go to the Gentiles, and they [the Jerusalem Community] would go to the Jews." In fact, Peter not only accepted Paul's theology — and Peter knew Jesus personally — but he also joined the mission to the Gentiles, moving to Rome.

This is not to be read as if Paul had "taken over the Church." On the contrary, Paul had taken his case to Jerusalem to get their judgment. Still, the "ordinary Christian" was not merely the object of a decision, but an active agent in resolving the Church's common problems. This happened again later over the question of observing the Jewish dietary laws, and again the Church changed its mind.

As Paul Johnson says in *A History of Christianity:*

Paul did not invent Christianity, or pervert it: he rescued it from extinction. ... Paul moved right across the religious conspectus, from narrow sectarianism to militant universalism, and from strict legalism to a complete repudiation of the law — the first Christian to do so: not even Jesus had gone so far.

Not only did these decisions avoid a schism between Jewish and Gentile Christians, but they freed the Church from its seedbed in Israel and called it out into the world — the Remnant on the road, as Yahweh had summoned Noah, Abraham, and Moses. Luke saw that decision to cut the Church from Judaism as an event equal to Jesus' decision to take his ministry up to Jerusalem, even though he knew it meant his death. The infant Church was on its way to becoming "catholic," a Church with open arms.

In the year 70 A.D., the Romans destroyed the Temple in Jerusalem and ended its influences on the Christian Church forever. A large number of Jerusalem Christians dispersed into other countries of the empire. Again, providence was forcing the Christian Church to become a "catholic" Church.

The Gospel according to Paul

It is good to remember Paul based his faith not on the flesh-and-blood Jesus the Apostles knew, but on the risen Jesus he experienced. Moreover, his written testimony is chronologically the earliest we have of the new Christian myth.

As Peter is the focal disciple in the gospels and in the early sections of Acts, now Paul, the missionary and theologian, takes a central role in this emerging Church. Among Paul's many contributions (the greatest of which was opening the Church to the world and preventing it from being reabsorbed into Judaism), there are three that essentially affected the way the Church was growing: his extraordinary skill in probing the implications of the message of Jesus and expressing it in his letters, his confrontation of the problem of enthusiasm vs. discipline, and his meditation on the Church as the embodiment of Christ.

Paul authored what is the most far-reaching correspondence in history; there has never been anyone else whose letters are still read, every week, by millions of people all over the world. In those letters (most of which were written earlier than the gospels), we can actually see the Church growing: The earlier ones show a Church waiting impatiently for "the day of the Lord," a literal re-creation of the world; the later ones show a Church resigned to the fact that God had other plans, not a Kingdom of marble and bronze but a Kingdom of the heart.

Paul was not, in our sense, a Church "official," like a pope or a cardinal. He was a new kind of "authority": a theologian. His job was unraveling the message compacted into Jesus' mustard seed, to make explicit what was implicit in it. In his meditations on Jesus' message, Paul displays the two characteristics of a great thinker: respect for the traditional, essential truths, coupled with a willingness to think them anew, to adapt them to situations Jesus had not envisioned — and yet without violating their normative spirit. Here we find, again, that basic principle of the Church: once you have grasped the essentials, everything else is, at least to some degree, negotiable.

All histories are a record of controversies, and that is surely true of the Church's history. We have already seen the disputes over circumcision and dietary laws. For Paul, another problem arose, to which Jesus had given no answer, and Paul had to answer it the way Jesus would have. This was the conflict between Christians who wanted the Church's practices to be filled with joyful enthusiasm, and those who wanted them disciplined and reverent. It would be misstating the case to say this early controversy parallels the difference between present-day charismatics and those who feel at least "uneasy" about charismatics' ways of worshiping, but Paul's handling of this conflict between enthusiasm and discipline could give food for thought to both viewpoints. It is also not without insights into fundamentalism.

I said before that anyone who genuinely has discovered the Kingdom ought to have the same reaction as someone who found a treasure in a field: "Holy [*beep*]!" But each of us is different — a fact that keeps stories interesting and history filled with controversy. Not all of us respond in the same way. Some wear their Christian conversion on their chests, like blazing badges; others keep their conversion as a quiet source of energy within them. Nor is baptism magic. Pouring water on someone and saying some words, however inwardly transforming, doesn't turn a shy person into a world-beater or a glad-hander into a quietist.

Moreover, there are two kinds of spirits: the Holy Spirit, who is a true source of inspiration, and — for want of a better term — the Evil Spirit. By that term I do not mean to imply (or deny) a disembodied, wicked, intelligent being who goes around whispering evil thoughts and plots into our ears. But at the very least, like the term "original sin," it serves to denote a fact that is beyond dispute: Not only do human beings mess up, but they can convince themselves that in fact they did *not* — and they were really acting under the inspiration of the Holy Spirit. So, at least for the moment, let "the Evil Spirit" stand for that undeniable, self-defensive human propensity to justify an action that is, objectively, evil — and even argue that it is good.

One element in the early Church manifested its enthusiasm for the gospel by jumping around, shouting out, and talking in what they claimed to be "tongues": messages from the Holy Spirit expressed in no known language. But there are a whole range of enthusiasms, ranging from the "high" of being forgiven at a Billy Graham rally, to the "high" from the spirits that come out of a bottle, to the "high" a psychopath feels on a murder spree.

We will encounter this same problem later when it breaks out again in Gnosticism, the first of the great heresies. Its adherents claimed to have a secret "inner vision" that was self-authenticating and needed no logical foundation. It is a "gift" given only to a chosen few, and all who dare to question its validity are held in contempt. Anyone who has ever been trapped in an argument with a born-again Christian has no further need of explanation about what Gnosticism means.

Faith does take more than just disciplined thought and careful, left-brain arguments. It requires intuitive, right-brain insight as well. Faith is calculated, but it is also a risk. A Christian needs not only the discipline of a reasoned moral code, but he or she also needs to shed shyness and manifest the faith enthusiastically: as Jesus said, to climb to the housetops and shout the Good News.

Paul faced this conflict between disciplined reasoning and inspired insight, very dramatically, in the city of Corinth. It was a cosmopolitan center of government, business, and commerce, and its moral tone can be guessed from the fact that "a Corinthian girl" was a common name for a prostitute. The problems of the community were not that different from the Church's problems in a culture that is strongly influenced by *Playboy*, Madison Avenue, burned-out ghettoes, state-funded abortions, and crack.

One extreme faction of the Corinthian community became wildly enthusiastic about their new-found Christian insight, especially their ability to speak in tongues. Seized by religious fervor at the Eucharist, they would shout incoherent words interspersed with "Abba! Alleluia! Come quickly, Lord Jesus!" Much of this is found today in Pentecostal sects and to some extent among charismatic Catholics. On the surface, it is not at all unlike the enthusiasm at a rock concert.

How does someone judge the reality of any kind of experience if he or she has never had it? How can one outside the experience judge whether this is an authentic outpouring of spiritual joy, or merely self-indulgent, self-deceptive raving?

In no way did Paul forbid enthusiast activity in the Corinthian community (which alienated the more conservative faction), but he did insist on discerning the *source* of this inspiration, to determine whether it was Holy and beneficial to the whole community or Evil and self-serving (which alienated the enthusiast faction).

Paul's norm to determine that source of the "gift" was the norm Jesus gave us: "By their fruits you will know them." If the enthusiasts felt a Gnostic superiority to anyone not so "gifted," if they believed that they themselves were the only true Christians, then their disdain and contempt was evidence enough that their inspiration was Evil. The test of all gifts is love. Jesus had said, "By *this* will they know that you are my disciples: that you love one another." If the "gift" resulted in greater love, then it truly was a gift of the Holy Spirit; if it resulted in smugness, insulation, and contempt, it was not a gift to the Church but a curse.

Neither excessive enthusiasm nor excessive strictness characterizes the Christian Church. There is room for all: Jew and Greek, male and female, enthusiasts and quietists. The crucial question is *balance.*

The quotation from Chesterton on the page vii continues:

> It was no flock of sheep the Christian shepherd was leading, but a herd of bulls and tigers, of terrible ideals and devouring doctrines, each one of them enough to turn to a false religion and lay waste the world.

As Peter and Paul had prevented a schism between Jewish Christians and Gentile Christians, Paul prevented a schism between enthusiast Christians and quietist Christians. Not only is there *room* in the Church for all different types of people, but there is *need* for their — balancing — differences. This he pursued further in his analogy of the members of the Church as different parts of Christ's Body. The Church itself is the Body of Christ, energized by his spirit.

The message of Jesus is a message of love, even for sinners. That love erases all former ethnic, social, and religious barriers that human beings think divide them. And all grudges. In the Body of Christ, the Christian Church, no single member — except the Spirit of Jesus — is essential, but every member is important. No member is more important than any other; all members are equal. And yet even though each of us is equal to any other, each of us is also unique, each with a contribution to be made to the whole that no one else can offer.

> God put all the separate parts into the body on purpose. If all parts were the same, how could it be a body? The parts are many, but the body is one. The eye cannot say to the hand, "I do not need you," nor can the hand say to the feet, "I do not need you. . . ." If one part

is hurt, all parts are hurt with it. If one part is given special honor, all parts enjoy it. (1 Cor. 12:18–21, 26)

The Body needs each of us, with his or her special gifts, without which the evolution of the Body would be lessened. Thus, the enthusiast cannot say to the quietist, "I don't need you." On the contrary, each very much needs the other — to correct the Body's balance. Neither the pastor nor the person in the pews can say, "I don't need you." Nor is either more important than the other; they just serve different functions in the Body. Nor do any two pastors or any two lay people serve the same function. The qualities of my personality have been an actual obstacle to some people's discovering what I most want them to discover: "the liberty we enjoy in Christ Jesus." Fortunately for them — and for me — there are many other priests; somewhere there is one whom the Goldilocks Method will prove "just right."

Therefore, as Paul says, each one must "try to discover what the Lord wants of you," so that each fulfills himself or herself to the fullest, *in* Christ. The first step (which is one of the major purposes of education) is to discover just what your human gifts are. Then you can offer those gifts to the service of the community. So many people I know are so afraid of "being used." And yet, in order to be useful, you have to be used!

At every Eucharist, we offer ordinary gifts — bread and wine — and we ask our Father once again, by that great miracle, to infuse into those gifts the living presence of Jesus Christ and, through them, infuse that living presence into us. The Body may be ungainly, mistake-prone, anything but ideal. But it is a Body animated by the Spirit of Christ. And we've seen, again and again, what our Father can do with the unlikeliest bodies.

~ Questions for Discussion ~

1. Paul answered the problem of how to judge someone else's experience "from the outside" by invoking the principle of Jesus: "By their fruits you shall know them." You can legitimately judge someone else's claims that his or her inner conviction is true and genuinely wholesome only by witnessing what effect that conviction has on that person's everyday behavior in other situations. Does that conviction, in practice, make the person more loving, less judgmental, more honest and open and free? Or does it make him or her more ill-tempered, less tolerant, more dishonest and secretive and self-limiting? Does that conviction come from the Holy Spirit, who is Truth, or does it come from the Evil Spirit, which is self-deception?

Apply Paul's rule-of-thumb to the perennial problem of two people who are in an extra-marital sexual relationship, when they are sure that this is "the real thing" and their parents and friends are not quite so sure. How could you tell from the couple's relationships outside their own that their belief really is the truth and not a self-deception? What would be *concrete*, specific examples of behavior rooted in a very good relationship?

2. The chapter also spoke of the doctrines of the Christian Church as being not all of uniform importance. Some doctrines are essential, some are consistent with the core of essentials but conditioned by a particular time and culture, and some are clearly aberrations from basic Christian doctrine, even though a large number of Christians held them as true, and often for quite some time. The divinity of Christ, the resurrection, and the Eucharist are obviously essentials; circumcision, the universal Latin Mass, and eating fish on Friday were culturally conditioned and not essential; the Inquisition, the papal states, and warrior-bishops were aberrations.

List all the doctrines of the Christian Church that you believe are very likely essential, that is, without them a particular community could not legitimately call itself "Christian."

Chapter 8

Who's Got the "Right" Jesus?

O N THE ONE HAND, perfect uniformity is unnatural, something for mindless Nazis. On the other hand, perfect non-conformity is equally unnatural, something for mental wards. Both are unnatural because they deny the function of the human mind: to think for oneself as a unique individual, and yet also to think honestly and logically, searching for the truth rather than merely "winning." To have a perfectly closed mind, incapable of change or doubt, is to be dead-brained; to have a perfectly open mind, committed to nothing, is to have an empty head.

It is essential to keep remembering Chesterton's image of the Church as a rock of nearly infinite facets, each one making its unique contribution, and yet each one also acting as a balancing corrective to its opposite. There is a single unifying principle, the spirit of our common myth: the Person of Jesus Christ. That spirit not only unifies us but also sets us free to make our unique contributions. We are neither slavish automatons, nor are we free-floating blobs.

The left lobe of our minds was made to categorize, but the right lobe was made to invent, to discover, to have new insights. The left brain is — or ought to be — a willing slave to the truth: humbly bowing to what is, rather than forcing it to be what it is not. The right brain is totally free: exploring what-is-not-yet, dreaming, pushing beyond what other men and women have considered the fixed horizons. If all of our left brains were equally clear-sighted and honest, all our ideas would be the same: statements about what is. But if all of our right brains were uniform, we'd all be back in the caves or dead of boredom.

As a result, in a sense, there are as many "Christianities" as there are Christians. Just as no two children see their parents in precisely the same way, no two Christians see Jesus — or read what he wants them to do — in precisely the same way. There are not merely "liberal" and "conservative" Christians, but a whole spectrum of Christians. Where is the hard line, for instance, between a "conservative" and an "arch-conservative," or between a "liberal" and a "radical"? Our minds want categories as sharp and clean as cookie cutters, but reality — especially people — won't surrender to them. We have charismatic Christians, Marxist Christians, exuberant and stodgy, flamboyant and shy, enthusiasts and quietists. And they're all Christians, even though their eyes trade dagger-thrusts when they meet.

We do not want, and fortunately cannot have, perfect uniformity in any institution, any human embodiment of a myth. The question arises, however: When does a viewpoint or practice or belief break completely away from the unifying spirit of the myth? No question here about the sincerity or honesty of the dissenter; he or she could be a saint. But when does a person cease to be, truly, a Christian — becoming perhaps even a heretic?

A pause to consider the word. "Heresy" and "heretic" were once used as weapons. For centuries, they were enough to send someone to be burned at the stake. And the word was flung around with great abandon: St. Joan of Arc was burned at the stake for "heresy," as were many other obvious saints. Great minds hurled the word back and forth like grenades. Before Vatican II, it was accepted practice to call Protestants "heretics," which is pretty insulting for starters, and disquieting for those whose own relatives are mostly Protestant. Now we refer to Protestants in less condescending terms. They are our "separated brethren." I restrict the word "heresy" here to the way it is used still in most history books: a doctrine the universal Church deemed in violation of an essential of Christ's doctrine. All the heresies discussed in this chapter are heresies to Protestants as well.

Nobody's been hauled to the stake recently for refusing to give up Adoptionism; in fact I doubt if too many educated Christians could say what it means. But almost every week I hear someone say, "Well, Jesus was a fine moral teacher, but that's all." Which is *precisely* what Adoptionism means! People who say Jesus was "just" a fine moral teacher like Gandhi may sign "Christian" or "Catholic" when some printed form asks for their religion, but they're not. They deny Jesus was God.

Heresy denies some element of the faith that the Church deems essential if the believer continues using the word "Christian" about himself or herself — and most especially if he wants to continue to preach or be a bishop. In denying the divinity of Christ, for instance, Adoptionists negate Christianity's very core. That doesn't mean they should have their tongues cut out, nor that they are not kind, hard-working, generous people. They're just not Christians, any more than one could have denied racial superiority and remained a good Nazi.

This is one of the main reasons why a serious Christian needs an organized Church, an ecclesiastical structure with a good working relationship between its professional decision-makers (pope and bishops) and its professional thinkers (theologians). Not that people in the pews don't have a right to an opinion, but determining whether some new opinion, first, *is* an essential, and, second, *is* actually violated by this new "movement" takes more expertise than most in the pews care to acquire. We're not talking about birth control, or homosexuals, or abortion. We're talking about stances regarding Christian doctrine that may be denials of the core of Christianity.

Ideally, the relationship between the decision-makers and the theologians (on both sides of any disputed question) should be fair, unprejudiced by a like for someone's politics or economics or a dislike for someone's ethnic background or parentage. There should be both freedom and discipline, enthusiasm and control, and the decision-makers should be both normative and flexible.

Unfortunately, it rarely — if ever — is. In the simpler days of the apostolic Church, Peter could quite likely have been just such a judge. But with the rapid expansion of the Church, there were simply too many pots the decision-makers had to have their fingers into. And there were many, many proponents of solutions on a whole range of questions, and each with an axe to grind. And use. Quite often to lop off a great chunk of the Church. The shepherds were not herding sheep, but lions and tigers!

A Church of Theologians

For most of the Church's history, including today, the ordinary believer has been content to tend fields, diaper babies, and let the famous fret over theology. Today, about the only point of doctrine that could cause heavy argument might be about the official Church's stance on birth control. But there was a time when "everybody was a theologian," and a passionate one!

At that time, bishops apparently really knew how to preach, to make clear even points of doctrine that would cross the eyes of a seminarian. Or at least they could rally do-or-die support to their own point of view. Without television, newspapers, or even books, the Sunday homily and the conversations after it were "The News of the Week." As a result, theological questions stirred ordinary people the way today only the fortunes of the hometown ball club could. The butcher, baker, and candlestickmaker shouted one another down about the most obscure points of doctrine, and often with clubs and paving stones!

Jesus was not a theoretical theologian. He proclaimed a message, not an encyclopedic, scrupulously detailed theory. As he left shepherding and administering to Peter, that is, to the decision-makers, he left unraveling the fine print and unanswered questions of the gospel to Paul, that is, to the theologians. What kind of being was Jesus, anyway? How is Jesus both human and divine? And if both Jesus and the Father are God, how can there still be one God? And where does the Holy Spirit fit in? Is she God, too? And where does that leave us? Has Jesus changed what being human means by becoming one of us, dying, rising? How?

Each age puts new questions to the gospels. And, among human beings, varying interpretations and explanations can lead to fist fights, or schisms, or even wars. As questionable opinions began to spread, councils of bishops and theologians from all over the known world gathered to examine the conflicting interpretations in the light of reason, tradition, and the mind of Jesus as manifested in the gospel.

Nor were these council meetings the sedate, polite, apparently serene gatherings you might expect from seeing a film about Vatican II. Both sides obscured the issues: by their human faults, their need to dominate, tactlessness, national pride. As with speeches from either side during any political campaign, it's difficult to separate the truth from the rhetoric — on both sides. Despite the fact many participants in the debates have been made saints and are hallowed in history books, they resorted to underhanded tricks, bribery, and often baseless attacks on their opponents' morality as well as their opponents' doctrines. And their opponents did likewise, the "heresiarchs" (arch-heretic leaders), who were not only genuine in their beliefs but quite likely, before a Higher Judge, worthy to be called saints themselves.

What's more, even when the question at issue was (tentatively, more or less temporarily) "settled" by the majority of bishops, nearly every rejected opinion still had its adherents, and, as we will see, many of those heresies condemned by the Church are still alive and well today — in the minds (however unwittingly) of many otherwise pious and practicing Catholics.

A heresy always begins well: with an important truth the Church, especially the official Church, has long been ignoring in favor of its opposite. The leaders found a common resentment among the people; they saw which way the parade was heading and simply got in front of it, gave it a focus and a voice. They were responding to what we now call "popular demand," as in "When is the official Church gonna do something about . . . ?"

Questions that get the more bitter inner juices of the decision-makers and theologians in the Church working overtime seem to the ordinary Christian merely a tornado in a toilet, yet they can have a profound effect on the ordinary believer. For instance overstress on the divinity of Jesus makes Jesus beyond imitation, a perfection beyond the capacity of a fumbling, fallible, and finite Christian. Or, on the other side, our laudable attempts to understand Jesus as a human being, close and accessible to us (like the Adoptionists) can make him "just one more really good guy," and therefore deny that he could be the source of a divine life in us. When someone is overstressing, someone else is out there getting ready to cry, "Heresy!"

Heresy is, as with all single-mindedness, a tragedy triggered by the best of intentions, a vice evolving from a virtue: like truth unchecked by charity, charity unchecked by common sense. Left-brain scientism or right-brain superstition take over and become gods. No balance. It is for that reason that, despite their unpleasant surface overtones, the councils of the Church have struggled to remain universal, to avoid one-sided answers. That's what a heresy is: a one-sided, one-lobed answer.

The heresy of choice in our own do-it-yourself age is, hands down, *Pelagianism,* the winningest — and perhaps first-ever — heresy in the history of humankind. It thrived long before there were Church councils, or even a Church, or even dictionaries. In fact, Pelagianism *is* the original sin: "Who needs God? I will eat this and become equal to God. I can do it alone! I'll *do* the job — if only God'll just get out of the way and let me!"

Whatever you may hold about the first time that cussedness entered human history, the sin of Adam and Eve is the skeletal outline of every sin that followed it. It is at the core of every one of the wanderings of Israel from Yahweh, the boast of Oedipus and Jocaste, the Prodigal Son, the Macbeths — and you and me: "Who needs God?" That's Pelagianism.

Often, incautiously, even the wisest believe that Pelagianism — "I can take care of it *myself!*" — results from arrogance. From my own submission to it and from my experience of it in others, I tend to doubt that. I think it has more to do with loneliness than with arrogance. Pelagianism is not merely the conviction that "I *can* go it alone," but that "I *must* — because I *am* alone."

In 418 A.D., a gathering of two hundred bishops at the sixteenth Council of Carthage condemned the errors of the British monk Pelagius, who insisted salvation is possible without grace, through human effort alone. In fact, he said, if there is such a thing as grace, it is the original gift of human intelligence and will, the ability to cope and to overcome. Pelagius, rightly, cherished freedom. He just cherished it too much, just as the Reformers (at least as the Council of Trent understood them) respected human freedom too little.

In effect, Pelagius took human history out of God's hands, as Adam and Eve tried to do. As each of us has tried to do.

Pelagius was partly right. Humans are not born totally vicious because of original sin. We ought to apply the corrective of common sense to the ancient understandings of sin that go all the way back to the narrow-minded, puritan Tertullian in the second century of the Church: a debt incurred by the human family to some divine and merciless moneylender, some inner spiritual virus passed down in the human soul through sexual intercourse, making infants who are not yet responsible for their own toilet habits somehow sinful. But Pelagius and his well-intentioned disciples negate the need and perhaps even the existence of any kind of supernatural dimension to human living. Again, negating an essential. If there is no Fifth Dimension, Jesus is just one more good guy.

In a book of Church history, the uproar over Pelagianism seems to be no more than a squabble over whether to break your soft-boiled egg at the big end or the little end. But such ideas leak out of the ivory tower into the marketplace, just as Freud unknowingly paved the way for Hugh Hefner (whom he quite likely would have despised), and Galileo unwittingly begat Carl Sagan.

There is probably no "megatrend" in our present society stronger than its adoration of self-improvement, invulnerability, and macho competition. You prove yourself, ransom your soul — your self — by capitalizing on the opposition's weakness. The "value" of a society or an individual is immediately evident from the scoreboard, the Gross National Product, the bank balance. You know from the TV, the Little League tryouts, the report card, the SATs, what you're *really* "worth." "I did it *myself!*"

If that's your myth, your idea of your real value, you're a secret Pelagian. No need to search for the cause of so many teenage suicides. The cause is rampant Pelagianism: unrealizable expectations of what human life and one's fellow human beings — and one's self — can deliver. The only answer is a humble one, but also a liberating one: "I don't have to do it alone, because I'm not alone." But to do that, you have to allow God his place, and you have to discover your true place in relation to it.

The genuine Church is a tightrope walker. It needs balance. Problems — like heresies — arise only when either the left extreme or the right extreme rejects the corrective counterbalance of the other, when we stare at the truth with only one eye instead of two. Many tire of the nerve-wracking task of walking the wire, correcting a bit to the left, a bit to the right all the time. They weary of what they often feel is "pussy-footing," so they jump — to right or to left. It's certainly a definitive move.

But it's always disastrous.

The leftist (rationalistic) heresies, from Simon Magus to Carl Sagan, are overly left-brain. They attempt to eliminate mystery and restrict themselves to what reason can comfortably grasp. The rightist (anti-intellectual) heresies, from the early speakers in tongues to the present-day fundamentalists, are overly right-brain. They throw up their hands in the face of the Impenetrable and reduce the questions to as few as possible.

Heresies on the left work "from the bottom up." They are more immanent (this-worldly) at the expense of the transcendent (other-worldly), emphasizing the accessible humanity of Jesus even at the expense of his divinity. Where rightists speak of the Word *"taking flesh,"* leftists focus on the Word *"becoming human."* The difference may seem like just splitting pine needles, but it is such differences that can become calls to battle.

"Taking flesh" has connotations of a perfect and pre-existing Being putting on a kind of uniform of humanity that signifies his unity with all others who wear that uniform — but that in no way changes him internally (the otherworldly Jesus you see in biblical movies). "Becoming human" connotes something intrinsic: Jesus did not merely "put on" humanity, like a garment; he saturated himself with it, even its "less dignified" aspects like sexuality, even to genuine doubt, the one anguish no animal or angel is capable of (the down-to-earth Jesus you find in the much-debated *The Last Temptation of Christ*).

Viewed from the left, Jesus is the Jesus of history, who shared our work and walked our ways, sweated, felt sexual desire, doubted, died, rose, and was exalted. This is the aspect we find more (though not exclusively) in the Gospels of Mark, Matthew, and Luke. The more otherworldly side of Jesus emerges strongly in the Fourth Gospel and in Paul, after the message had spread into the more sophisticated Greek-thinking world beyond Palestine. Both are valid, necessary insights. Together.

Leftist Heresies

The leftist heresies are most clearly understood through the Jesus of *Jesus Christ Superstar:* as Mary Magdalene sings, "He's just a man." (Few audiences realize that, although all the other actors in the show take a curtain call, "Jesus" doesn't.) It is not that they are untrue to aspects of Jesus, it's just that they eliminate what they find confounding: not an expression of open falsehood but a suppression of truth — which is in itself a kind of falsehood. Like a compass reading just a few points off the course, they tend to compound their error the farther they go.

Adoptionism, as we saw, simplifies the whole question of who Jesus was: a very good man, so good that God adopted him as his firstborn, the first fully evolved human being.

Arianism in the fourth century said something similar but more subtle: The Word was the first entity God *created,* then through him God created everything else. But the Word — who ultimately became Jesus — was still a creature, like us, but far greater. The Father must exist *before* he expresses the Word. Therefore, it was not Jesus who redeemed us but God who redeemed us, *using* Jesus as his instrument.

According to the Arians, the Son is like God (of *similar* substance), but is not the same nature as God (of the *same* substance: "one in being with the Father"). Here, too, we are not dealing merely with theological niceties. If Jesus was not God, then it was merely a very good creature who died on the cross. God did not become one of us, did not offer us the last leap in evolution: a share in the aliveness of God. Moreover, John says, "The Word *was* God, and Word was made flesh and dwelt among us."

Nestorianism edged further back toward orthodoxy but hardly all the way. It claimed there were two *distinct* persons in Jesus, one divine and one human, almost as if the divine Jesus "possessed" the human Jesus. Thus, it was not the divine God who died on the cross, but the human Jesus. It was not the human Jesus who redeemed us, but God. Mary was not the Mother of God, but only the mother of the human Jesus.

For centuries, the leftist, intellectual heresies faded before the by-no-means leftist leanings of the Inquisition. But with the Protestant Reformation, the French Revolution, and the dawn of the Enlightenment (the ascendancy of cold rational thought over the vulnerability of faith), many thinkers began to argue that any proposition should not merely be accepted because some decision-maker said it was true but because it could be proved inescapably true from reason alone. *Deism,* which thrived in the eighteenth century, held that there must be a Mind Behind It All, but that mind is, essentially, unknowable.

Many went further and declared that since the supernatural cannot be grasped at all by the left brain, it should be left to the puffery of poets and priests. Not only is God essentially unknowable, but there is no *need* for a Mind Behind It All: Atheism, and also a special brand of atheism known as *Scientism* (as in Carl Sagan), asserts that no supposed entity can lay claim to reality unless it can be in some way verified by scientific apparatus. That mind-set is captured in the Apostle Thomas, when he said he wouldn't believe until he could put his fingers into the supposedly risen Jesus' wounds. Every religious ed teacher faces that mind-set every day in class.

As the more scientific literary methods spread into the study of scripture, scholars began to see that the New Testament is not a dispassionate historical account of the life and message of Jesus but, rather, an account written by highly subjective members of the early Church, often reading back from their own times and having Jesus deal with issues that weren't even issues in his time, perhaps even putting words into Jesus' mouth.

As a result, in the nineteenth century there arose a new heresy called *Modernism,* which was roundly and repeatedly condemned by the Vatican. At its most extreme, Modernism was resolutely anti-dogmatic, anti-traditional, and anti-transcendent.

This is as good a place as any to point out another case of simplism that is as common in the Church as it is in the world of politics: painting with the broad brush, lumping together into one broad "bin" what is actually a whole variegated spectrum of related but quite different positions. Single-(simple-)minded political figures with painful frequency slap the label "Communist" or "Marxist" on any opinion or movement even slightly to the left-of-center, so that fire-breathing guerrillas, spies, proponents of welfare for the helpless, and even nuns teaching the gospel's concern for the rights of the poor are all "Leftists" and, ipso facto, "Communists." It simplifies things. The only problem is that it's utterly false. Yet, because of such simplism, nuns and priests were murdered in El Salvador.

The same thing happened with Modernism. Anything smacking of innovation — or even intellectualism — became suspect. As we will see, between Vatican I and Vatican II the official Church took on at least a resemblance to the unlamented Inquisition. With an irony frequent in history, Modernism's excesses stalled the advance of even what was true in it and shrouded even honest theological progress under the label "Modernist."

It generated a kind of counter-heresy: authoritarianism, so despised by St. Paul and so foreign to "the freedom we enjoy in Christ Jesus." The official Church became a kind of watchdog against intellectualism, withdrawing teaching credentials from any suspect professor, producing the Index of Forbidden Books (in which many entries today seem laughable), requiring that every priest before ordination take a public oath against Modernism, warning (like the Jewish Temple) avoidance of any contamination from Jews, Protestants, Freemasons, and a host of others, teaching theology in seminaries from manuals in which any not-strictly-orthodox opinion was dismissed as ludicrous in a single paragraph, demanding that children (and college students!) memorize a catechism they didn't remotely understand, and at least suggesting that the ordinary Christian, even with an advanced degree, was not capable of reading scripture and in fact in danger of getting heretical notions by reading it. Thus began a century of Catholic theological and scriptural illiteracy.

But the Church cannot lean too far to right or to left for too long without capsizing and shattering. With a further irony, many of those formerly dumped into the Modernist "bin" emerged as invited experts to Vatican II, and many of their doctrines were accepted as the opinions of the universal Church. When he had been teaching at the Bergamo seminary, even the later John XXIII was suspected of being a secret Modernist!

The Church of Vatican II realized (1) that dogmatic definitions, even the best-intentioned, are always inadequate to their Object: God; (2) that Jesus' revelation went first for the heart and only then for the head; and (3) that the gospel is a scroll only gradually unfolded.

However, she did not run pell-mell from absolutism into the arms of the relativist opposition. She realized, still, (1) that definitions — even at the moment inadequate ones — are not useless, but essential for understanding and communicating, (2) that Christians are not merely hearts but also heads, and (3) that the scriptures are not documents to be understood *only* by the trained biblical scholar. We are not just the Church today; we are a Church with a two-thousand-year story.

Nonetheless, the Jesus of the modern liberal remains almost solely the liberator of the poor, female, gay, black, and unpropertied. Yet, that is only half the picture, Jesus seen only from his left side. Although he was neither rich nor a sinner, Jesus had a demonstrated empathy for both the rich and for the sinner. As bad as the sugary Jesus of the holy cards, this is a selective reading of scripture, because Jesus said he did not come to abolish the Law but to renew it.

Rightist Heresies

The rightist heresies can be understood from Greek orthodox church art, majestic and somber depictions of Jesus of heroic size, penetrating gaze, and near absence of anything resembling human emotion. He is also the Jesus of films more "reverent" than *Superstar,* like Zeffirelli's *Jesus of Nazareth:* pale, otherworldly, his embarrassing humanity *absorbed* into his divinity, like a wrong hushed-up, Jesus as the tubercular, blue-eyed Goy, an Oxford professor slightly put-off to be caught slumming.

If leftist heresies insist on Jesus' total embrace of humanity, even of its "less dignified" aspects, the rightist heresies withdraw Jesus in exactly the opposite direction, especially in regard to that least dignified of human qualities: S-E-X.

You can trace the roots of this incomplete idea of Jesus — and therefore of God and humankind — all the way back to Plato, who had such a strong influence on the early Church as it emerged from Judaism. Plato says in *The Republic* that sexual desire is a "diseased" aspect of the human personality. The scholastic theologians from the Middle Ages up through the Modernism scare and into this century referred to the sex organs as *res inhonestae* ("shameful parts") and even to normal nocturnal emissions as "pollutions." Thomas Aquinas argued for the Immaculate Conception of Our Lady because "original sin comes from the male seed." In the resultant art, therefore, Jesus is sexless.

This is the Jesus who merely "took flesh," as if holding a garment at arms' length and turning his face from it, as if it were something that might contaminate his divinity. This Jesus is a far cry — emotionally as well as theologically — from *Superstar* or *Godspell.* The embarrassing tempest over the Katzanzakis film *The Last Temptation of Christ* comes from the far right. If the novel and film go overboard to the left, their critics at least seem to be leaning way too far to the right.

Nor is this merely a theological or literary debate. The *psychological* results of treating Jesus — and therefore the nature of God and the nature of human beings — in a way that is too otherworldly has been humanly devastating; it is widespread and continues unabated. You can see that the questions underlying debates over heresy are not merely some kind of "celestial calculus" engaged in only by eggheads. There are profound effects in a Christian's life. In preserving Jesus from human "pollution" and "shameful parts," heretics on the right have created unnumbered unnaturally scrupulous psychological wrecks.

Heresies on the right work "from the top down." They are more transcendent, emphasizing the inaccessible divinity of Christ at the expense of the humanity of Jesus — even though sharing that divinity with us was precisely the reason Jesus had come! Unlike the Jesus of the left, the Jesus of the right does not submerge himself in humanity; his very person seems to defy the culture and pass woeful judgment on it.

Many of the rightist heresies have at least their logical roots in

Manicheism, although, again, their adherents may never even have heard the word. With many resonances to Eastern religions like Buddhism, Manicheism held that the flesh is evil and therefore Jesus could not possibly have embraced it fully. He could not have felt sexual temptation, much less undergone an uncontrollable nocturnal "pollution." Nor, they maintain, in direct contradiction to the gospels, could Jesus have had genuine empathy for sinners or genuine delight in food and wine.

The earliest rightist heresy in the Church was *Gnosticism,* which we saw briefly when considering St. Paul and the Church of Corinth. Gnostics insisted on an exaggerated role of knowledge in the individual's acceptance of salvation — not the clear logical knowledge of the rationalist, but a far more intuitive, objectively unverifiable gift of insight. This saving knowledge is a gift given only to few and, as I said before, anyone ever accosted by a born-again Christian needs no further explanation.

Gnostics, then and now, distrust theologians; orthodoxy is what counts; faith is enough, and intelligent curiosity seems something of an aberration. Gnostics' faith has less truck with reasoning than loyalty. Outside strictly religious questions, it is those who lay claim to this unchallengeable inner "light" who become witch-burners and fag-bashers and Commie-hunters. It also works at higher levels, when all those who question are suspect.

It is of such notions that *Puritanism* was born, the conviction that Church membership is restricted to those free from sin and that, outside that "elect" group, there is no salvation. This is, also, in direct contradiction to the gospel parable of the wheat and the weeds, the attitude of the Father of the Prodigal Son, and the fact that every one of the first Christians deserted Jesus and yet were welcomed back.

This is true also of *Jansenism,* which arose in seventeenth-century France, spread to the Irish seminaries, and thence to the United States. Like the other rightist heresies, it is elitist, bent on absolute moral uprightness, suspicious of anything purely natural, especially of sex, and notoriously intolerant. Jansenists fiercely opposed the Jesuitical practice of casuistry, arguing each case on its own unique merits against a firm but flexible background of reasoned principle. Such was the practice of the Pharisees, they said, and led inevitably to situation ethics.

Jesus from Both Sides

Jesus is the God-Man. As a result, our image of the nature and personality of Jesus mediates to us not only the nature and personality of God, but also our relationship to God: what is good and what is evil. If our image is overbalanced to the side of Jesus' humanity (the left), God seems so understanding that he becomes a spineless irrelevance, and our lives become equally irrelevant. Nothing we do, virtue or vice, makes any difference. If our image of Jesus is overbalanced to the side of Jesus' divinity (the right), God becomes distant and harshly judgmental, and we are at one and the same time both insignificant as insects yet sinners of unspeakable magnitude.

Both are in direct conflict with the gospel. The God Jesus speaks of and the God Jesus embodies is neither a Warm Fuzzy, just "one of the guys," nor is God a Hanging Judge, just watching for us to take one false step. The unique insight into God that Jesus gave us was: the Father, Abba, "Papa." A good father is neither a pushover nor an autocrat. Neither is God.

It is difficult for us to grasp the truth that: Jesus was both, with equal intensity: God and man, lion and lamb, serpent and dove. He gave up his divine powers and his realization of them, and relied, as we must, on the power from his Father. The carpenter who sweated and felt frustration and was accused of being "a glutton and a drunkard" was at the same time the Word through whom all was created. He spoke with authority, yet he never compelled assent. He invited the Rich Young Man to become an Apostle, yet loved him no less because he didn't feel free to accept. He hated what was wicked in his culture, yet he loved it enough to work for it and die for it.

Like Adam and Eve, we are uneasy with paradoxes and grab for a quick resolution, whether it is fruit from a tree or a guru or a heresiarch: just make it easy. Tell me I'm Oedipus, the monarch of all I survey. Or tell me I'm Sisyphus, the victim of a cruel and capricious Fate. We are uneasy being *both:* creatures, but nonetheless Peers of the Realm.

Yet we ourselves are living paradoxes, fusions of immortal spirit and transient flesh, fusions of agony and ecstasy. Until we are comfortable with paradox, and therefore with less than total certitude, we must remain grasping this half-truth or that half-truth. Unless I read the gospels incorrectly, the only thing I find Jesus "anti" was hypocrisy — which is just another name for smug certitude.

That is perhaps the key: humility, not before the iconoclast or before the inquisitor, but before the Truth.

~ Questions for Discussion ~

1. As well as you can, describe what the word "God" means to you as an individual, from your own personal and unique perspective. Then, describe what the word "Jesus" means to you as an individual. Finally, what effect does what you see God is and what you see Jesus is have on what you see *you* are? Then, if you can, swap your descriptions and discuss them.

2. The chapter made a strong case that most people today are infected with Pelagianism. Reread that section and see what concrete evidence you can come up with that would deny that assertion.

Chapter 9

Our First Thousand Years, 70–1054 A.D.

T HE STORY OF OUR TRIBE — the New Israel — is the story of a precarious balancing act. These next two chapters are only skeletal outlines of the most important events in Church history, rough, pre-Columbus maps. But they might lure you on to an encyclopedia or even to a history of Christianity.

St. Paul said that in the Christian Church "there is neither Jew nor Greek, slave nor free, male nor female, for you are all one in Christ Jesus." That is a statement of fact: we *are*, indeed, all united and equal in the Body of Christ. But there is a difference between a fact and an individual's or a particular culture's awareness of that fact. What we want to be fact becomes more important than any "fact." Just as Israel often forgot the essential truth that she was Yahweh's Chosen, the Church has often forgotten that she is Christ's Bride and has become what Israel so often became, a *casta meretrix*, "a chaste whore."

The Church has had many triumphs, not only a monumental influence in evolving and civilizing humankind, but in ennobling the lives of uncounted millions of "nobodies." Despite Paul's declaration, however, the Church has owned slaves, belittled women, executed Jews, divided itself into Roman and Greek, and waged wars in the name of the Prince of Peace. What's more, its decision-makers and theologians too often have forgotten that Jesus' norm for entering the Kingdom was the simplicity of a child and that he was constantly irritated at his disciples' yearning for power. Often, the Church has been divided into the Church teaching and the Church taught; the Church powerful and the Church powerless.

The Spirit is divine, but the Body is human. The Church shares the world's fate, the world's fallibility, and at times the world's corruption. She influences the world, and is influenced by the world. What follows then is the story of that back-and-forth interplay between the City of God and the City of Caesar. But it is also the story of the Church's own inner battles with herself, between the "chaste" ideal and the quite often "whorish" reality. Like anything human, the Church is never perfectible. But she is always and endlessly *improvable.*

As we progress, keep your eyes peeled for situations that occurred hundreds of years ago yet still recur today. Watch their "fruits" to see whether those occurrences then — and their recurrences today — are rooted in the Holy Spirit or in the Evil Spirit. See where we in the Church today may be veering from our myth, our ideal: the way Jesus would have handled problems that couldn't have been foreseen in his time. One pattern is clear throughout our years of balancing: when the Church gets into bed — or battle — with Caesar, she has forgotten what she is for.

A Church of Martyrs: 70–313 A.D.

The Roman Empire into which Christianity was born out of the womb of Israel was not unlike the world today. The comfortable pagan people in the suburbs practiced the basic human virtues: fidelity, tenderness, obedience, honesty. They observed the ordinary feasts of their gods, but, as today, it was a rather surface commitment, and their celebrations were more partying than praying. Intellectuals defended the Roman gods as little better than a way to keep good civil order. Their "religion" didn't touch the heart or make real demands on their willingness genuinely to commit themselves. None was fool enough to believe the emperor a god; their "worship" of him was no more sincere than paying taxes. Also, as today, the wealth of cities drew the poor from all over the world, seeking "a better life." They were packed into ghetto tenements riddled with filth and crime: prostitution, slavery, drugs, divorce, suicide, wholesale abortion — and a bewildering array of astrologers and fortune tellers.

Rome was a world of hedonist materialism, haves and have-nots, more or less at peace (*Pax Romana*), with a relatively stable government, yet a world without a center, a soul. As we saw with the "saints" of the present-day pagan myth, materialism just can't deliver what it promises. As with our own day, with its non-religious, humanist consciousness-raising gimmicks, pagan Rome was always on the lookout for some new Eastern mystery cult with the answer to the ultimate human question, which was put well in a song of our own day: "What's it all about, Alfie? Is it just for the moment we live?"

But the exotic Eastern mystery cults could not satisfy that natural human hunger for the transcendent either. Something in human nature cannot be becalmed for long by "a god." There is a hunger to lay hold on "the God."

Midway through the first century A.D., a new mystery cult from the East made its appearance in Rome. And with remarkable speed, many pagan Romans found it "just right." Within the first seventy years, there were thirteen Christian communities in Rome itself and small pockets all over the empire. Why? How?

Why? The appeal of Christianity, at first predominantly to poor folk (the "outlaws"), but also to a small number of aristocrats, is obvious. First, it cut across all lines of caste and social station. But beneath that, at its heart, Christianity dealt with three needs rooted in what being-human means in any time or culture: the need to find a reason for the unfairness of death; the need for a myth to give meaning to one's life; and the need for communication and love that is truly human and not merely an animal's contentment with the herd and with physical coupling. Christianity answered all three of those needs. For the Christian, death is the beginning of a new, true, eternal, individual life. The Christian has found a personal ethic in the myth of Jesus: You are the sons and daughters of God, and thus his royal agents: *noblesse oblige.* And the Christian enters an organic union with all other Christians and with the immortal God, the Body of Christ, energized by his Spirit.

How? Paul had wisely founded his seed communities at centers of government, commerce, and culture: Ephesus, Antioch, Corinth, Rome. From there, the Word radiated out along the trade routes. This interaction resulted in the mixed blessing of *syncretism,* the cross-feeding of ideas. An Apostle could explain Jesus to a Jew by saying he was the fulfillment of Isaiah's prophecies. But that did no good with a Gentile pagan; it forced the Church to "translate" her message into the symbols and thought-patterns of a different culture, which can result in far richer insights. But the message also runs the risk of being diluted into something aberrant, or even of being misread and contorted.

Romans got along fairly well with Jews, who were not actively seeking converts from paganism. When the Christians first arrived, they were similarly tolerated as one sect of Judaism. But the Christians had a mission: to baptize all nations. Christian businessmen and soldiers refused oaths by the divinity of the emperor. In areas of high Christian concentration, there was difficulty selling meat sacrificed to the gods. There were rumors that the "flesh and blood" of the Eucharist was a euphemism for cannibalism and the "kiss of peace" a euphemism for orgy. When pagan sons, wives, and slaves began to be converted from the family gods, there was bound to be trouble.

The Diaspora Jews around the empire numbered more than four million (compared to about one million in Palestine). While the Jews "at home" tended to be poor, backward, and closed-minded, the Diaspora Jews were generally well-to-do, cultured, and open to new ideas. Thus they were likelier candidates for conversion than their more fundamentalist Palestinian relatives. The Romans admired their skill in business, their ethics, their close family ties, and their endlessly tolerant system of "welfare" — at least for one another. But the Jews were also an integral element of the Roman economy, and, as we will see so often, economics and politics are almost always "more important" in decision-making than the niceties of theology, no matter whose theology.

On one hand, because of their Jewish roots, Christians found an affinity and a fertile field for conversions among some Jews. But on the other, no matter how cosmopolitan Diaspora Jews might be, to the vast majority these Christians were heretics from Judaism, no better than Samaritans, a corruption to be uprooted.

Thus the Christians became an ironically unifying element between pagan and Jew: they were a common whipping-boy. "And from that day, Pilate and Herod became friends."

On the night of July 18, 64 A.D., a devastating fire broke out in the overcrowded city and ravaged every district for six days and nights. The dead were uncountable. When it was finally controlled, eleven of fifteen districts were uninhabitable. The Emperor Nero could not discover who had caused the fire (quite likely not without looking into a mirror). What better scapegoat than the one group all factions hated already: the Christians?

Thus began an orgy of informing and betrayal — which, tragically, nominal Christians themselves would later repeat in the name of religion: the Inquisition, the Salem witch trials, the Holocaust. Christians were tortured, beheaded, crucified, sewn into animal skins and hunted, soaked in pitch and set afire to light up Nero's garden. One of his many victims was St. Paul.

For the next 250 years, in great spasmodic waves of persecution and peace, Christians were hounded into the long night of the catacombs. In underground burial labyrinths in Rome, Sicily, North Africa, and Asia Minor, Christians furtively gathered to strengthen their own threatened faith from the shared faith of one another in the Eucharist. It is difficult to imagine yawning through a liturgy in a catacomb, or leaving one's Christian principles behind in that one short period a week. The Church is never stronger than when it is persecuted — as witness the Church in Eastern Europe after nearly half a century of suppression. Despite the iniquity of the persecution, the one word archaeologists find most often in the graffiti of the catacombs is: "Peace."

At this time, the Mass was a simple ceremony: readings from the Old Testament, Paul, the gospels, a homily, a prayer, hymns, followed by a kiss of fellowship and distribution of the Bread and Wine. By the time of St. Justin Martyr (100–163?), it had become an absolute obligation for the orthodox Christian.

In the records and letters of this same time, the outlines of Church organization in the now much-expanded community become clearer. Each local church had its supervisor (bishop), elders (a priest-senate), presbyters (priests), and deacons, chosen by the community for their wisdom, holiness, and leadership. As early as 106 A.D., a letter of St. Ignatius of Antioch refers to the community at Rome as earlier letters had referred to the now-dispersed mother community of Jerusalem: "the president of the brotherhood of the faithful." Because it boasted not one but two Apostles, Peter and Paul, to link it to the mother community, it became known as the "Apostolic See" (jurisdiction).

And yet, as early as the end of the second century, Origen, the first great philosopher to rethink the nature of the Church, not as an extension of Judaism but as an entity of its own, accepted an absolute distinction between clergy and laity and portrayed the Church as a kind of "spiritual State" with its own princes (priests), kings (bishops), and emperor. One or other of the two Spirits was getting them ready for Constantine.

Despite the persecutions — and because of them — the mustard seed was beginning to flourish.

A Church of "Authorities": 300–500

In the year 312, after a revelatory experience not unlike St. Paul's on the way to Damascus, the Emperor Constantine was converted to the truths of Christianity. The following year, in the Edict of Milan, he decreed religious toleration of all faiths. A complex man, in whom paganism and politics warred with Christianity, he was still an ardent protector of the Church of the Martyrs. He produced legislation applying the principles of the Christian gospel to the human needs of his people, especially outcasts. He reputedly revised the method of dating from A.U.C. (*ab urbe condita*) to A.D., pivoting around the birth of Christ rather than the founding of Rome. Christian festivals began to replace pagan ones; pagan shrines began to disappear. The Church was merging into the main society as an officially recognized institution.

Constantine tried to do exactly what Jesus had asked: to make the family of God coextensive with the human family. He considered himself a minister of God, administering the renovation of humankind. Just as Christ rules in the name of his Father, Constantine — like a new David — rules in the name of Christ. Obviously, this results in a Church and State very closely interwoven, and it was even more true in the East, after Constantine had moved his capital to Byzantium (now Istanbul).

At least that's what the history books have said until recently. Constantine delayed his baptism till his deathbed; the reason, the older books say, is that he wanted to make sure his sins (and they continued to be many) were really "wiped out." But even after his conversion, he didn't abandon sun worship, and when he moved his capital to Constantinople, he erected a heroic-sized statue to the sun god and made Sunday the day of rest.

Constantine was bizarre but no fool. Christians had become far more numerous, especially in the army on which Constantine depended. Christians had extended their welfare services, not only to their own but to pagans. Christian-bashing was no longer a popular sport. Unlike the Jews, they had no nationalist focus. And there is evidence Constantine admired the Church's literate clerics, that he wanted a state/church in which those clerics would be clerks. And, according to his friend, Bishop Eusebius, Constantine had read Origen's description of the Church's hierarchy — which almost perfectly paralleled Constantine's own.

The great councils of this time tried to answer the essentially unanswerable: How could Christianity be a monotheism and yet still have a Father, Son, and Spirit, each of whom is divine (Nicea, 325; Chalcedon, 451)? These issues excited more passion, in councils and in the streets, in the Eastern Church centered around Constantinople than in the Western Church centered around Rome, partly because Greek, the language and mind-set of the Eastern Church, was capable of far more subtle distinctions than was the relatively rustic Latin of the Western Church.

But it also underlines two opposite sides of the Balancing Rock that continue to make legitimate demands on the Church through our history to today. Jesus' Church is "catholic," universal, open to all. This means a meaningful place must be found in it not only for male and female, rich and poor, right and left, but also both for peasant and intellectual. It cannot become merely exorcisms, superstitions, and relics for the revivalists, and celestial calculus and historically correct liturgies for the eggheads. One is tempted to see in the new liturgy a total pendulum-swing from the majestic Latin crowd-pleasers of pre–Vatican II, to a stripped-down, historically accurate liturgy that leaves the ordinary folk snoring in the pews. When the Church tips too far toward the God of the theologians, it often loses focus on the Jesus who spoke of bread and wine, hidden treasure, and juvenile delinquents coming home.

Just the opposite of our recent veering away from pomp and circumstance was happening in the Church near the death of the empire. Damasus, Bishop of Rome (366–84), spent a great deal of money to integrate the Church into Roman and imperial culture, to make Christianity more appealing to unconverted pagans, to provide lukewarm Christians with a faith more attractive than lingering pagan cults, and also to increase support for his claims that the Bishop of Rome was the obvious successor to St. Peter. He had his secretary, Jerome, translate the scriptures into people's Latin and Latinized the Mass. Damasus regretted no money spent to suffuse Christian ritual with grandeur: gold vessels, marble, canopies, candles, incense. Priests and bishops donned the tunic and toga of Roman senators, which have since become the alb and chasuble. On one hand, we had come a long way from the stable, Upper Room, and catacombs — which had been just fine for Jesus and the early Church. On the other, that sense of majesty is an element — non-essential, to be sure — that many younger Catholics have never known, and that many older Catholics sorely miss.

In reaction against such worldliness, Damasus's secretary, Jerome, retired to a monastery in Palestine, tirelessly writing — and wrestling wretchedly with the sexuality in his flesh and with most other physical pleasures, like food, clothing, relaxation, which are not only perfectly natural but a part of a fulfilled humanity. Like Tertullian before him and Augustine after him, he seemed driven to *suppress* the wolves of his sexuality, rather than making peace with them, taming them, and harnessing their power. These men's pessimism about the way God made us has little connection with the joyful proclamation of Jesus or with the freedom Paul says we enjoy in Christ Jesus. But all three were great men who made incalculable contributions to the Church, yet all their preachments were accepted by the unwary as of equal insight. Thus, these three giants not only enriched the Church but did irreparable harm to the psychology of good Christians and to the credibility of the Christian message for two thousand years.

After Jesus and Paul, no other person gave the Church a sense of herself and her purpose more than Bishop Augustine of Hippo (in Algeria). Like all the other Fathers of the Church we have seen, he was a gifted, tireless man, whose character was such a menagerie of contrary movements that he is both elusive and fascinating. Augustine's life bridged the years from the pagan persecutions through the invasions from the North and the collapse of the empire.

Augustine's mentor was Bishop Ambrose of Milan, a superb administrator, baptized as an adult and eight days later consecrated bishop. In Ambrose's concerns, the greatest seemed to have been "power," and not just spiritual power. He did not like the idea of married bishops, not on sexual grounds, but because their sons might inherit their positions and power; if a married man in Ambrose's jurisdiction were made bishop, he could have no more children. Working with Ambrose, Augustine saw what a superb institution the Church was capable of being: the City of God enlivening the City of Man — the total Christian society.

But, Augustine reasoned, if it is the will of God that all be saved, then no one has a choice but to enter the City of God, not even well-intentioned heretics, like Pelagius. Hadn't Jesus "coerced" Paul at the time of his conversion? Without discipline, there is chaos. Thus the Church has the right to censorship, secret police, informants, and threats of torture. If the well-run state did it, why not the well-run Church? The Church had come from being the persecuted to a potential persecutor. The first known instance of a Christian witch hunt slaughtered the heretical Bishop of Avila in 385. It was "a cloud no bigger than a fist," but it would grow nearer, and darker.

As with all syncretism, the patronage of Constantine was not an unmixed blessing. Making friends with Caesar was — and remained — one of the most perilous threats to the precarious balance of the Church. What's more, it was to affect not only the visible nature of the Church but all Western history to this very day.

Constantine built churches to rival pagan temples, huge, lushly ornamented houses in which the historical Jesus would hardly have felt at home. Priests and bishops began to involve themselves in imperial government, in order to "go in their door and lead them out ours." Unfortunately, more than a few were seduced by the perquisites of power and stayed inside.

Individual church officials from now on had to resist the temptation to imitate the authoritarianism, centralization, and bureaucracy of the State — not to mention its pretentious uniforms, which often give an outward show of a power that may be missing within. No longer could Peter say to the cripple, "Silver and gold have I none, but what I have I give you: take up your bed and walk." No longer was inner conversion necessary; when barbarian chiefs were converted (for various motives), all their tribe was baptized with them. Before, being Christian had been a crime; now, not being a Christian was ever so gradually beginning to be a crime — or at least quite imprudent.

Syncretism can be enriching, yet it has also always been a potential threat to the precarious balance. From Judaism, Christianity gratefully accepted its monotheism, its Messiah, its scriptures, its very roots; yet we are also always in danger of the same overemphasis on legalism that so troubled Paul. From Greece, we gratefully accepted a profound humanism, a common language that facilitated the spread of the gospel, the great philosophical insights and methods of thinking of Plato and Aristotle; yet we are also in danger of becoming too left-brain about the gospel, losing its ability to move the heart in a tangle of intellectualism. From Rome, the Church accepted a reprieve from persecution, an institution based on clear lines of authority to care for an enormous number of people, yet we are also always in danger of empty formalism and repressive authoritarianism.

Constantine's transfer of the imperial court to his new capital in the East also had its good and bad effects. On one hand, it freed the pope in Rome from a somewhat suspect imperial "protection." On the other, the move gave the formerly obscure Bishop of Constantinople a meteoric rise in stature. The Church was in danger — and not for the last time — of having "two popes."

In the second century, the Church had developed the sinews of an ecclesiastical organization; in the third, it began to rough out and then focus its philosophical and theological understanding of itself; and in the fourth, it began to embody itself before the Christian and non-Christian "public" as an institution to be reckoned with.

Then the empire collapsed.

The Dark Ages: 450–1000

Imperial Rome — and its Church — were now under threat. Waves of invaders swept through Europe from the East and the forests of Germany — Visigoths, Vandals, Huns, whose very names have become synonyms for rape and destruction. They broke down the very centralization that had made the empire possible, a breakdown that later became the separatist nationalisms we know today. And the Church, who had "married" the empire, came very near to collapse, too. But she didn't. If the law of "the survival of the fittest" applies also to human societies, the Church proved remarkably fit, despite her many mistakes.

But it was a profoundly upsetting time. Try to imagine America invaded by roving armies from the jungles of the Amazon or from outer space, sophisticated in astrophysics but profoundly puzzled by anything right-brain. And the story of the next five hundred years details how the Church conquered those conquerors.

The conquerors acquired lands and wives and began to adapt their customs and their language. But they were faced with administrative chaos. All the officials who had held the social structure together were killed or fled. The road system, and therefore also commerce, was in ruins; whatever roads remained were infested with outlaws. People were starving. Government no longer existed, and the newcomers weren't much interested in that sort of thing; tribal government had served them well enough. Yet they had to contain the chaos or risk uprisings and losing all they had conquered. So they turned to the only systematic institution they had: the Church.

Gradually, the bishops, through their literate clergy, more or less ran the cities. The "machine" was already in place, with records, without which no organizing bureaucracy can exist. In a way, the very "legalism" that seemed so alien to Paul was what, in effect, saved the Church. And nowhere was there a stronger bureaucracy in place than in Rome. Pope Gregory I (the Great) at the end of the sixth century was a tough, practical man who had been civil prefect of Rome. He was also a man who bowed before the truth rather than manufacturing his own: "The [Roman] eagle has gone bald and lost its feathers. Where is the senate? Where are the old people? Gone." There was no time now for doctrinal niceties. He set to work with what was, for survival.

The Church was prepared to collaborate with the invaders not only for its own future, but also for the survival of the *past*. At the moment, the Church had more or less a monopoly on literacy, and literacy is the key to the solutions from the past. Monks in their scriptoria not only copied out the ancient texts, but they also shrewdly wrote the new tribes' histories, or rather "rewrote" them, so that the invaders' arrival at Christianity now appeared to have been the plan of Christian Providence all along.

Monks living in community were nothing new. All the way back to the Jewish Essenes, men and women of religious fervor (ranging from genuine sanctity to sheer spiritual lunacy) had fled to out-of-the-way places, as Jerome had done, to escape the materialism and hypocrisy of "the world." But in 530, on the nearly inaccessible crag of Monte Cassino in Italy, St. Benedict founded an order of monks whose rule was common sense — a quality often lacking in the history of the Church, even in our own day.

The Benedictine Rule was a balanced interplay between freedom and discipline. In *all* things — food, clothing, furniture, work — the monks' life was "adequate but simple." Exceptions were made for individuals. It was a classless society, in which the elected abbots served as the leaders

of the early Church had: spiritual leaders, decision-makers, but not am-
bitious bureaucrats (for a long while). They were not "of" the world, but
neither were they divorced from it.

The monks were marvelous managers. They worked hard, they were
disciplined, eager to invent new and better means to cultivate their lands.
They lured men away from (inefficient) slavery and serfdom. When they
were broken by the new Viking invasions, they started over. But above
all, the monks kept *books*.

Schools for training literate monks survived and, as they brought in
lay workers, they began to train literate laymen, too. Just as later the Jesuits would "back into" education instead of converting the Muslim, the
Benedictine farmers found themselves educators. But they needed more
books, so monks began copying the classics. By about 520, Boethius, a
layman, had translated all of Plato and Aristotle from Greek to Latin
(at the time, only the Irish monks still knew Greek), and the monks
sat in their scriptoria every day, preserving the story of the West, often
written in languages they themselves could not even comprehend. The
process was painfully slow; any library with even a hundred books was
considered a treasury.

In a hard age, when superstition by far dominated rational thought,
the magic power of relics was a major factor in the Church's acceptability,
especially to the barbarians. As Paul Johnson says, they "radiated energy
like a nuclear pile," and churches where they were housed were a source
of that protective energy. They were the motive for pilgrimages, fairs,
and, of course, trade. Grave robbers had a field day, coming up with
"genuine" bits of every saint back to Moses: More than a few heads of
John the Baptist, Our Lady's milk, her wedding ring, the tablecloth from
the Last Supper. It was real right-brain time.

Just as Bishop Eusebius had been advisor for the Emperor Constantine, Alcuin of York became the mentor of the man who would be the
next emperor of the West: Charlemagne, king of the Franks. Alcuin
was a Saxon, descendant of invaders, head of the palace school, an abbot,
who filled Charlemagne's mind with visions of the City of God. Charlemagne built schools because he needed a literate clergy to convert and
control the disparate tribes of Frisians, Saxons, and Slavs. Already his
kingdom was becoming at least nominally Christian, and Charlemagne
had higher ambitions. The last Western emperor had died in 478; on
Christmas, 800, Charlemagne was crowned Emperor of the West.

For centuries, the unity of the Western Church centered on Rome, in
devotion to St. Peter, but the power of the bishop of Rome was now min-
imal. Bishops were elected in dioceses far away, and Rome was merely

informed, though individual bishops often wrote to Rome rather than to their own archbishop. But as Charlemagne gradually unified the empire around himself, the Church (at least in the West) began to focus itself around the bishop of Rome, who began to command the same kind of ceremony about his person as the emperor. But Charlemagne was "the anointed of the Lord," and — because of the civil functions of bishops — he began appointing them not only to their civil offices but to their Church offices. Slowly, the Church became as feudalized as the State, with a hierarchical structure in which each lower level pledged its allegiance to the next higher level.

In about 580, on the other side of the world, a young Arab visionary named Mohammed had arisen with a simple religious creed that had united all the wandering desert tribes into a single force: Islam. Borrowing heavily from Judaism and Christianity, its view of God was rigidly monotheistic. Allah decrees your role in life, so work in it without complaint; to try to advance or change your station is, equivalently, blasphemy. A simple code of external ritual justified believers with Allah and enjoined on them the obligation to propagate their creed by Jihad, Holy War. Within ten years of its founder's death in 632, Islam had captured by force the entire Persian Empire, Syria, Palestine, and Egypt. By 711, it had subjugated all North Africa, Spain, and southern France. In less than a hundred years, the Church lost at least half its followers, and the Church of the West was completely cut off from the Church of the East.

Matters between the Bishop of Rome and the Bishop of Constantinople had never been better than hypocritically cordial. In the thicket of misunderstandings, there is no hope of laying blame on either side. One of the most important causes of collision was the confusion of terminology in the two quite different languages. But, at least theoretically, the major clash was over the insertion of one single word into the joint Church's creed: "Filioque."

The term "Filioque" signifies that the Holy Spirit proceeds from both the Father and the Son, just as the human spirit, the soul, results from a fusion of body and mind. But the Greek-thinking Church believed that term made the Spirit less than the Son, who proceeds from the Father alone and thus made the Spirit subordinate to both.

At rock bottom, however, the cause of the rift was antagonism over the authority of the patriarch of the East and the authority of the pope of Rome. Blinded on both sides to their basic brotherhood, by the very desire for power that Jesus so clearly condemned in his own disciples, in 1054, the Eastern half of Christendom went its own way in what is called the "Great Schism." Each side claimed to be the authentic

Kingdom of Christ and called the other side the "renegade." Although attempts have been made over the centuries, particularly recently, to heal the breach, to all intents and purposes the Body of Christ was divided against itself and remains so to this day.

Questions for Discussion

1. The chapter speaks a great deal about divisions between groups within an initially unified society. List as many causes of such divisions as you can. Then apply them to your office, neighborhood, or school — not only as a political union (administration, faculty, students, staff) but also as a sociological union (a group of human beings working together for, one hopes, a common purpose). As we've seen, union profits everyone. What are the things that divide your particular union? Which of them can be "healed"? How? When?

2. The chapter speaks of Darwin's "survival of the fittest." There is another law, this time from physics, called the Law of Entropy, which hypothesizes that everything, including the universe itself, has a tendency to sag back into uniform inertness. In other words, things wear out, fall apart, come unglued. As we have seen, that law applies also to human societies, e.g., the Roman Empire. What elements within the Church have served to keep the Church — astonishingly — alive, despite that law?

Chapter 10

The Second Millennium

I N THE OLD TESTAMENT, there is a very puzzling character named Melchizedek; his name comes up at Mass sometimes, "You are a priest, according to the order of Melchizedek." But Melchizedek had a very tough job. He was both the high priest and the king. That makes for tough decisions, like a Catholic American governor or legislator faced with a choice between the Supreme Court's reading of the Constitution and his or her conscience on the issue of government funding of abortions. Who answers the question: the king or the priest, the elected official or the private conscience — when they're both the same person?

In the first thousand years of Christianity, both the Church and the State were monarchical: prince/priest, king/bishop, emperor/pope. They were like two parents: they had the same job — to instil godliness, harmony, and peace — and the same children to guide, protect, and set free to live adult lives. But sometimes there were good kings and bad popes, and vice versa. When both were good, there was a chance that everyone would profit. But when one parent "wins," everybody loses. The same thing is true of management and unions. Or Church and State.

When we read history, we tend to strip the participants to their naked, heroic roles — as we do watching the "Tonight Show." We forget that these people, whether Charlemagne or Cher, put on their socks one at a time and have axes to grind, just as we do. Whether it's a discussion at your dinner table, or a gathering of bishops, or a meeting between a bejeweled emperor and a satin-clad pope, the question on the table is not always a matter of honestly finding the truth. The question is a matter of *power*, precisely what the disciples so dearly wanted and Jesus so definitively rejected in the very act of being crucified.

Just as at your dinner table, so also at the conference table, there are desires and unexamined convictions that are not about to be sidetracked by anything as inconsequential as the truth. Or by the greatest good for all concerned.

113

All the more when we have an interwoven *union* of two ecologies, as with Church and State at the end of what has been named the "Dark Ages." The Spirit inside that spiritual/civil Body of Christ is like a fire. Contained, fire is a powerful force; unchecked, it wreaks destruction. The same with the Spirit of the Church: If the Spirit is checked by too many rules, it grows listless and corrupt; if the Spirit is left unchecked, there is chaos. The human psyche hasn't come that far from Paul and his Corinthians. Or from the caves. More polite, perhaps, but no less eager to come out on top, and damn the damage.

When either side, or both, is not more concerned with truth, with the good of the members both of Church and State, but only with power, then there is only one way to resolve differences: force. When truth has no meaning, then, as Nietzsche said much later, "Might makes right." The emperor resorts to force: refusal to allow funds to leave his country for Rome, threatening priests and bishops, gobbling the funds of "his" monasteries. The pope resorts to force: excommunicating the emperor, interdicting subjects from obeying his orders. And when the clergy "work for" both king and pope, each is faced with a ticklish choice: a very painful and perhaps prolonged death here and now at the hands of the king, or an eternally prolonged death in hell at the hands of the pope. Real test of basic loyalties there.

It is the difference between a contest and cooperation. When any government — sacred or secular, international or familial — treats the other side as an "opposing team," when compromise becomes unthinkable and the argument becomes no more than propaganda and counter-propaganda, then you don't need a crystal ball to see what's ahead: misery. For everybody.

This is not the fault of the Church. Or the papacy. Or of any kingdom or government. It's the fault of imperfectly evolved human beings. The relationship between Church and State for the next thousand years is exactly like a couple always on the verge of a divorce — except in the number of people who get hurt.

Still, there have to be decision-makers, whether the decision is about heresy and morality or about taxes and war. And ordinary men and women who put their socks on one at a time have to make those decisions, under all kinds of real and imagined pressures and, being human, without a total knowledge of the truth. Nor is power a bad thing. Whether it is the power that comes from having money, or an army, or the keys to heaven and hell, or the threat of torture and death, power is what "gets things done." And we all want that.

The Early Middle Ages: 1000–1200 A.D.

The previous age was "Dark" only from one point of view. Actually, the "barbarians" had done the Church a favor: knocked her off the high horse on which she had been riding pillion behind Caesar and showed her what she really is: a servant. She moved back into a ruined society and rebuilt it. Then, again, just as with ancient Israel, when both Church and State had healed their wounds and begun again to consolidate their power, they began looking like divorce again. Thus, in a bewildering mix of "Benedicts" and "Henrys," each with his Roman numeral and his yearning to win, entropy moves back into Christendom.

Since bishops were literate and (supposedly) beyond corruption and (supposedly) had no sons to inherit their power, they seemed ideal administrators of the temporal aspects of the recovering State. But since the kings and emperors had a very vital stake in bishops' performing well, the State was allowed to select them, and quite often selected men known more for their ruthlessness than for their piety. It became a question of whether the pope consecrated the emperor, or whether the pope was merely the chief of the emperor's or king's bishops.

The struggle is embodied clearly in the film *Becket* and in T. S. Eliot's "Murder in the Cathedral." The treatment of the two principal characters, Thomas Becket, archbishop of Canterbury, and Henry II, king of England, depends again on one's point of view. Historically, the issue between the two former friends was: Which power had the right to discipline clergymen (who worked for both) when said clergy stole, raped, or murdered — which they did with embarrassing frequency. Unlike the fictional treatments, Henry was genuinely seeking a mutually agreeable compromise, but Becket was sternly unbending and — true to Eliot's play — as self-dramatizing as Hamlet. But the point for him was: the temporal power is subject to the spiritual power, and the spiritual power is subject only to God. All well and good for a cleric's offenses that harm his relationship with God, but what of those same offenses that harm his relationship with the State — and demand punishment?

Both questions — the anti-social activities of clerics and the power to control them — came to a head on the grand papal-imperial stage in the conflict between Pope Gregory VII (Hildebrand) and Emperor Henry IV, between an imperial pope and a pontifical emperor. When Henry, who was notorious for selling bishop's miters, refused to return the power of naming bishops to the pope, Gregory excommunicated him. But Gregory went further and, in an unprecedented act, deposed him from his throne and freed all his vassals from their oaths of allegiance — and their taxes. Even Henry's bishops deserted him, and on January 28, 1077, at the castle of Canossa, the emperor knelt in the snow at the pope's feet and begged his forgiveness.

It was a historical moment, but, like the patronage of Constantine, a triumph only from one point of view. First, Canossa began the long march to a sorely needed but mixed-blessing codification of Church law. Second, it reversed the loyalties of the Church/State clerks and made the empire unworkable — as if the union president were allowed to name all managers. The stronger the pope, the weaker his bishops. No one could judge the pope but God, yet, at least in theory, only the pope could say definitively what God's judgments were. Third, Canossa finally admitted the struggle was not on behalf of the people whom each side reputedly served, but rather in the cause of power for each side. It was not a case for truth — or even common sense — but for legal claims. This is a very long way from the Jesus who said that the vulnerability of a child is the way into his Kingdom.

The social commentator John Gardner said, "The first sign of a dying society is a new edition of the rule book." It is a sure indication that the spirit that first motivated the lacrosse team or the pick-up play is dead and that, if the operation is to continue, there have to be rules — and penalties (power). No society, however great or small, can survive *without* laws. But when fear of punishment replaces the Spirit, and when the laws proliferate like rabbits, the law becomes self-defeating.

Whereas the Spirit had once penetrated every element of a Christian's and a clergyman's lives, now the law took its place. It covered every last detail, not merely of the administration of the sacraments, but the rights, duties, and obligations of every parish priest and layperson: dress, crimes, punishments, alms, legitimacy, sex and morals, prayers. A bishop's care of souls gave way to adjudicating legal questions and mechanical administration and reports to Rome. The papal court (curia) became basically a legal tribunal, and for every theologian on the pope's staff there were twenty canon lawyers.

There is a real question whether the ordinary layman and laywoman really minded having a priest who was — visibly — no less a sinner than themselves. What they objected to in the (cruelly underpaid) clergy was their greed: tithes, death taxes paid before the deceased could have a requiem Mass, indulgences to avoid the humiliation of public penance; and much of those funds were sent back to Rome, which could hardly remain unbiased about them. In 1376, for instance, the House of Commons complained that each year the English clergy sent the pope five times the revenues of the English crown. Lay people began to equate "the Church" with the clergy, and thus it became "them," just one more tax-collecting agency added onto the king's tax-collectors.

Finally, however, when Boniface VIII forbade any king to tax the clergy, King Edward I of England and King Philip the Fair of France called the pope's bluff. Without those revenues, the kingdom would come to a halt. So Edward instructed sheriffs to seize Church lands, and Philip banned any export of currency — especially to Italy. Boniface countered with a decree of excommunication and interdict. But such threats are useless when those to whom they are addressed fear the king's present and certain punishment more than they fear the pope's future and perhaps negotiable punishment. Philip retaliated with charges of fraud, immorality, and heresy against Boniface and had him arrested. Two years later, Boniface's successor was taken off to Avignon in France, where the papacy remained — associated with only one country, without the symbolic identification with Peter and the Church's own true origins and purpose — from 1309 to 1377.

So much, for the moment, for politics. On the lower, less dramatic but more human levels, the Church was not all chaos. The centers of learning were moving from the country monasteries to the beginnings of universities in the cities. The new cathedrals, as all art, began to reflect a change in the spirit of the times, from Romanesque (like fortresses) to the airily reaching spires of the Gothic (like poems and songs). Statues were no longer the grim-faced, heroic Roman warriors but faces and bodies that bespoke pain endured, joy, even playfulness.

Even such an apparently insignificant change as the invention of the astrolabe signaled a new opening for growth, since it allowed sailors to move out into the open seas away from the protective coastland. Like their improving maps, they were unknowingly preparing for Columbus and Magellan.

In the growing university, the Church outside the monasteries withdrew from merely running around plugging the holes in the defenses and was beginning to find its mind again. In 1140, from the University of Bologna, came a definitive code of Church law by Gratian. From the University of Paris came *The Book of Sentences* by Peter Lombard, which would be the basic theological text of the Church for more than a hundred years until Thomas Aquinas. Peter Abelard began to apply the newly discovered logic of Aristotle to the study of traditional doctrine; he was one of the creators of scientific theology. Although some of the monks of St. Benedict were instructed in theology, during the entire Middle Ages right up to the sixteenth century, there were oddly no seminaries for training priests. Thus, the candidates for the priesthood from wealthy families were generally literate — and gravitated to the cities. Most country priests were ignorant men, although in theory they had to be literate. Some were even unable to translate the prayers of the Latin Mass.

New forms of religious life began to arise. St. Bernard founded the Cistercians, semi-hermits in wild marshes and heaths whose lives were dedicated to penance and atonement for sins and reclaiming much-needed farmland. In 1122, there were 19 Cistercians; in 1134, there were 70; by the end of the century, there were 530. St. Norbert founded the Premonstratensians, organized around a common life and just as strict as the Cistercians but with two differences. For the first time in the Church, study formed an integral part of spiritual life; research is a prayer to the One Truth, because unearthing the secrets of nature and of humankind is unearthing the secrets of God. But also the monks of St. Norbert moved out into the community to serve the people.

They were joined at the beginning of the thirteenth century by the Friars Preacher (Dominicans) and the Friars Minor (Franciscans), who took vows of poverty — thus negating the laity's distaste for money-grubbing clergy. Not only could no monk own anything personally, but the order itself refused to own anything.

Dominicans were originally from the upper classes, highly literate, and took as their task to explain orthodox doctrine in common terms among people confused by all kinds of heretical and quack sects. Unlike the Benedictines and Cistercians, who took a vow to remain in one house forever, the Dominicans were rather an army of priests, organized in provinces under a Master-General, and ready to serve wherever the need was greatest.

Franciscans came mostly from the lower classes, and for some time many were lay people and illiterate. Their apostolate was to the learned but to those who had become heretics, or were wavering in their faith, or morally corrupt — rich or poor. Later, especially when priests joined them, Franciscans began to attend the universities and teach at them.

The two new orders obviously responded to a felt need. At the end of a single century, Dominicans had 600 houses with 12,000 friars, and Franciscans had an astonishing 1,400 houses with 28,000 friars. Discipline in all the houses, even the least strict, was rigorous.

Despite its obvious missionary origins, it was not until the opening of China and India by Marco Polo and the New World by Columbus that the Church had any serious missionary activity or any specifically missionary order. Once the Church had "settled in" at the time of Constantine, she faced the dissolution of the barbarian invasions and was forced again to "re-evangelize herself." Then, rather than turn her eyes outward, she focused whatever missionary zeal she had on rooting out deviations in doctrine within Europe. Tragically, the only "missionary" movement of the Church outside Europe was the Crusades.

The First Crusade began in 1097 and, typically, Crusaders are more heroic in movies than in actual history. The First Crusade did regain the city of Jerusalem. It did arouse a unity of spirit throughout Christendom, renew the spirit in the clergy to some extent, and strengthen the popularity and unifying function of the popes. But, like any war, it leached to the surface all kinds of bandits, swindlers, hustlers, and quacks. As in Vietnam, dark-skinned people — even Christians who had been overrun by the Islamic invaders — were slaughtered obscenely. Later Crusades ran amok and even attacked and pillaged Eastern Orthodox Constantinople. In 1365, the last Crusade sacked the mostly Christian city of Alexandria.

The huge numbers of men, women, and children who went on the Crusades were less interested in freeing Jerusalem than in land. Europe was too crowded; opportunities were limited. Yet, when they finally settled in, they made no move to convert the Muslims; they were (foolishly) forbidden to intermarry; and within ten years they were nearly all dead. Again, the fear churchmen have had, through the Church's history, of *pluralism* — live-and-let-live, forgetting "us" and "them" — proved fatal. For centuries, the Crusades embittered both the Muslims and the Orthodox and made compromise, peace, and reunion unthinkable.

High Middle Ages: 1200–1400

With an ironic consistency, the keys to the future are often handed to us from the past. At the root of the incessant differences in the Church between orthodoxy and heresy, between pope and emperor and people, was the lack of some comprehensive theory against which to judge itself: a theology. The Church, however, did not need merely one more journey into the impenetrable nature of the Trinity. The Fathers and Councils of the Church had belabored that for centuries, without much success, and lost half her membership in the process. Nor did she need one more theory about the Church as a society. From Boethius through Augustine, the endless bickerings between Church and State had belabored that one, too, for twelve hundred years — with not much success. Nor did she need yet another edition of Canon Law. Such approaches to the nature of the Church touch only the will, not the mind and the heart. What the Church needed was not merely to understand herself, or herself in relation to the State. What she needed was a new, richer understanding of herself in relation to . . . everything.

And that she was given, even though her official representatives were as skeptical about the gift as the Trojans should have been when the nasty Greeks delivered them that big wooden horse. There was some reason for the official Church's cynicism, however, because this gift was also a gift from the pagan Greeks: the mind of Aristotle.

It appears that in the fifth century Boethius had translated only Aristotle's *logical* works, and since there was no doctrine involved, they were harmless. But now here were works from a major scientist and philosopher, about everything from frogs to the nature of God. What could a vulgar pagan know of such things? And the gift was even more suspect — and ironic — because the texts came from the very "perfidious Muslim" who had been Europe's enemy for over a millennium.

Unlike Plato, whose negative ideas about matter had such a profound effect on Augustine, Aristotle believed that both matter and spirit are good. Science is not interested in studying the matter, but the forms, the natures, not how this person differs from that person (because of their separate matter) but how all humans are alike (because of their common nature). When we discover that, Aristotle says, we will discover what will fulfill each nature, since every entity purposefully pursues its nature. But since everything is purposeful, then there must be a Purposer: the entity called the Prime Mover or the Uncaused First Cause.

Here was an encyclopedia of human knowledge, analysis of all forms of life, the physical universe, human thinking and human conduct, government, poetics. It was a complete study of what Christianity claimed to be, namely, the answer to everything, and every step of the way Aristotle's system was painstakingly rational. How could the Church ignore it? From about the time of the founding of the great University of Paris in 1205, Aristotle began to be debated and explained and brought into harmony with the Christian lifeview. That struggle of minds was to bring the universities into a position where they could wield a brand new kind of power, one that would make them a formidable ally or opponent to the Church and to the State.

Albert the Great (1200–1280) was a new kind of Christian: the total believer, the total theologian, but also the total scientist, convinced that true theologians could not be merely theorizers but had to ground their theories in concrete reality and validate them in actual operation. "By their fruits you will know them." And Albert was known not only for his work but for its results. His finest student and the most influential Christian theologian of all time, Thomas Aquinas, produced for Christianity what Aristotle had produced for Greece: the *Summa Theologica,* which gave a Christian answer for . . . everything.

Aquinas believed theology and philosophy were separable, that one could look at reality as a believer (theology) or as a non-believer (philosophy), and — since each had its peculiar vantage point — each could enrich the other. As with Church and State, there is no need for the two sciences to compete with one another; they are both seeking the same thing: truth.

Aquinas gave Christian belief a solid basis in painstaking reasoning. He proved that faith need not be in conflict with reason. Like every gift we have seen so far, it was a mixed blessing, its left-brain grandeur often smothering the legitimate insights of right-brain intuition. The God of Abraham, Isaac, Jacob — and Jesus — is quite different from the Uncaused First Cause, yet both are legitimate viewpoints, and each is healthily corrective of the excesses of the other, just as the "masculine" and "feminine" sides of Jesus balance one another.

At first, the official Church forbade the teaching of the pagan Aristotle. How could the message of Jesus be clarified by looking through the eyes of a pagan, perhaps even of an atheist? (The same uproar exists today over liberation theology, which tries to find insights into the message of Jesus from the writings of the atheist Karl Marx.) Controversy raged over Christian texts influenced in any way by pagan thinking. In 1277, the Bishop of Paris condemned 219 propositions, 15 of them Aquinas's, and excommunicated all who held them. Within weeks, the condemnation was upheld by the pope.

For a society founded on an earth-shaking, revolutionary idea, the Christian Church is quick to scowl at some new way of thinking that becomes popular, almost certain there's a heresy under every bed. (The United States, which was founded in a somewhat similar manner, is none too comfortable with revolutions anymore, either.) This is not the first time we've seen this extra caution, nor will it be the last. It will arise again with Galileo, Luther, Descartes, the Modernists, Darwin, Freud, Heisenberg. The *casta meretrix* is scrappily defensive at times. She is afraid to acknowledge that the truth can never be harmful to honest religion; only refusal to acknowledge and accept a truth or valid new insight can harm honest religion. But the Church is human; as each of us, she is victim of the two roots of "original sin": the narcissism that refuses to admit one has made a mistake, and the inertia that is unwilling to go back to the first wrong turn and start over again.

But also the Church does take time; she has a longer perspective than most this-world news commentators. Gradually, she applies the wisdom of Jesus — "By their fruits you will know them" — and also the wisdom of Gamaliel testing his own "heretics": "If it is of God, it will survive, no matter what we do." And Aquinas is now, by papal law, the "official" theologian of the Church. Theologians who were considered Modernists were experts at Vatican II. And Galileo, Descartes, Darwin, Freud, and Heisenberg are all taught in officially Catholic colleges. Almost inevitably the *casta meretrix* forgets she's just one more human being who puts her socks on one at a time and acts as what she is: the Body of Christ, which has no fear of genuine truth.

Duns Scotus (1265–1307), a Franciscan writing about the same time as the Dominican Aquinas, saw reality from a similar and yet different viewpoint, just as Plato and his pupil, Aristotle, had. Aquinas emphasized intellect: reason; Scotus emphasized will: love. It is not enough to know the truth; one must then choose the truth. He also saw a flaw in the Aristotelian-Thomistic idea of individuality: that it was merely matter that makes "this" chair this one and "that" one that one. Each of us is human, but in an utterly unique way. I am not just human, I have a "Bill O'Malley-ness" that no one ever had before. It is individuals we love, not essences differentiated only by their matter.

William of Occam (d. 1349?) had the distinction of being arrested for heresy before he even got his master's degree from Oxford. Even while Occam was under house arrest, Pope John XXII preached a homily that, because of the outcry of theologians, he was forced to retract. So Occam used the occasion to ponder that, if the pope could err in doctrinal matters, perhaps a Church Council should have authority over the pope. Occam was a logician, infuriated by anyone who went further than the evidence and honest reasoning would allow. He anticipated by seven hundred years a principle that won Werner Heisenberg a Nobel Prize: the principle of uncertainty.

There is nothing we can say with utter certainty. Everything we know, we know approximately; the best we can speak of is not dogmatic certitude but only a high degree of probability. God is not restricted by the limitations of our thinking, nor, as Job discovered, by our ideas of fairness. Our statements are limited by minds that cannot see the total truth, as God can. Thus, all our statements must be open to improvement. They are not dogmas, but hypotheses, theories. Occam opened the door to a natural science unafraid to be wrong, to learn, to stop and rethink. He offered the same method to the Church.

The Crusades were not ended only by their own inhuman cruelty, but also by an intrusion simpler souls might have read as "the Wrath of God": the Black Death, a type of bubonic plague that began in 1348 and swept through every country in Europe, attacking principally the young and healthy. Half the population of England was wiped out in a single year; in two years, 40 million people died. No single group died more than priests, which demonstrates their self-sacrifices for the victims and offers at least some corrective to history books that record only those clerics who ran afoul of the law, and therefore leave a reader with the impression that most priests in the Church's history have been womanizing illiterates.

But the Black Death did have disastrous results on the clergy. The places of the innumerable dead priests were often filled in haste by untrained and unsuitable men. And the plague went further. Much of the literature of the time seems to show a broken spirit; if anything can arise so unexpectedly and wipe us out, "let's break out the booze and have a ball, if that's all there is." The Black Death and people's responses to it are echoed today in our response to the possibility of nuclear war or a worldwide AIDS epidemic, each of which, perhaps even without our knowing, affects our attitudes and behavior.

With foreign crusades now considered at the very best ill advised, the official Church turned its attention to an internal "foreign threat": heresy. In 1230, the Vatican empowered a permanent tribunal, staffed by Dominican friars, who as we have seen were prepared to go anywhere the pope commanded. The Inquisition was, literally, above the law and above ordinary legal procedure: informants could remain anonymous, the accused was allowed no counsel, or even any defense, and there was no appeal. Everyone was required to take an oath to report heretics, and failure to receive Communion two or three times a year was automatically cause for extra watchfulness. If you tried to read the scriptures for yourself, you were courting trouble.

In itself, the work of the Inquisition was a despicable form of "thought control" and forcing of consciences — which Jesus had never done. What's more, it was a horrifying way for small-minded people to engage in petty vendettas. "A heretic is anyone who disagrees with me." Worst, since the Inquisitors had no scientific approach to criminology and obtaining logical evidence, torture began to be allowed as a means to the "truth" around 1400. Surprisingly, very few even of those judged definitely heretical were executed: less than 10 percent of those condemned. But every prison was soon filled to bursting.

As we have seen, the pope was a virtual prisoner of the French king at Avignon. Of the 134 cardinal-electors who chose the seven (French) popes between 1305 and 1378, 113 were French. When the remarkably young (forty-two) Gregory IX finally brought the papacy back to Rome, he died in little over a year (which raises suspicions) and an Italian mob gathered outside the Vatican shouting, "Elect an Italian or die!" The cardinal-electors dutifully elected an Italian — who was a tempestuous tyrant who may well have gone mad in the process. The cardinals escaped the city and four months later declared the election invalid and named a new pope. For the next forty years, the Church was presented with the problem of having two "popes" (at times three) since, as each "pope" died, a new group of cardinals elected a new successor in each line. It is all too deliciously complex to go into here, including a man who was quite likely the worst pope ever to pretend to the throne of Peter, the first John XXIII.

History books deal almost exclusively with the great players on the Church's stage or with the exceptional small-time players who become important by being — or being suspected of being — deviants. But by far the majority of the Body of Christ is the small-time people who live lives not worth the note of historians, like the people on Chaucer's trip to the shrine of Thomas Becket in *The Canterbury Tales*. Like Thomas Aquinas, Geoffrey Chaucer was a genius, but more of the right-brain than the left. He balances a healthy intellectual Christianity with a healthy "paganism," rooting Christianity in the earth, as its Founder had. In the High Middle Ages, Chaucer's pilgrims are the Church: honestly pious knights and priests, prayerful but bawdy widows, conniving sellers of relics and indulgences, naively worldly nuns, and so on. In their talk, sexual indulgence is something to remember, of course, but nowhere near as evil as the hypocrisy of pompous clerical crooks or the hard-heartedness of the unloving — the very people Jesus found repellent. Perhaps the great had lost the Spirit that sinewed together the Body of Christ, but a great many of the common folk had not.

Renaissance, Rebellion, Reform: 1400–1600

The world as Europe knew it was being reborn, its horizons cracking open. In the previous century, Marco Polo had extended the known world to the East, all the way to China, and in the fifteenth century, Columbus doubled the size of the world that could be known. And perhaps even more important, in 1455, in Mainz, the printing press offered the ordinary man and woman the unheard of opportunity of exploring the world of the human mind.

Just as Aristotle had offered the key to a resurgence in philosophy and theology, now the Greek and Latin poets and playwrights, artists and sculptors, opened up a whole new area of the human mind that had been stifled: the world of non-religious symbols. While the theologian tried to probe the mysteries of God, the artist tried to probe the mysteries of humanity. Alas, a good deal of what many believed to be paganism still clung to it. But the popes became eager patrons of art, establishing the Vatican Library and launching the new St. Peter's Basilica.

A good deal of what even pagans believed to be paganism clung to the papacy, too. The lives of many of the Renaissance popes were stories that would overload the circuits even of the *National Enquirer,* and their priorities in the task to which they had been elected were also frequently distorted at best. More than a few intended to use the papacy as a means to make their families into a new dynasty, carving out lands for them from the Papal States and appointing them to the papal court, no matter what their ages or whether they had troubled to be ordained. By 1500, some popes unblushingly acknowledged their own illegitimate children and bestowed on them Church office (and revenues) or used them to make advantageous marriages. They did this not solely out of family love. When poison is an integral weapon of statecraft, it's consoling to know you can (probably) trust the people who work most closely with you. But also, to give them some credit, it is good to know you have someone to count on when you want to "get things done."

It was not a time of which the Church can be in any way proud of its leadership, except for one or two of its (usually short-lived) popes. In a very real sense, the Apostles had finally gotten what they had kept badgering Jesus for: exactly the opposite of what he intended them to be. Yet for one who sees Providence working ever so patiently on an enormous canvas, the reasoning is clear: unless the Church could find itself at rock bottom, there was little likelihood of rebellion, and thus little likelihood of reform. That is the insight not only of Marxism but of Alcoholics Anonymous.

Neither of the usual terms "Protestant Reformation" or "Counter-Reformation" is without its flaws. "Reformation" might well describe individuals engaged in trying to bring the Church to its senses, but what they ultimately accomplished seems so different from what they set out to change that it seems truer to call it "starting over again." And "Counter-Reformation" implies that the Catholics who opposed the Protestants were opposed to any reform whatever. For some, that was quite true; for others, it was far from the truth.

Desiderius Erasmus (1466–1536) was a man-in-the-middle, caught between the forces of tradition and the forces of change, both of which he valued. A classical scholar and translator, arguably the best-read man of the age, his own books were being read all over Europe. As such, he was the focal figure of the New Learning. Technically a cleric, only because as a priest's bastard he had been forced into it, he considered himself a layman, trying to discover the truth. He tried to look at all texts — even the scriptures — with "new eyes," probing behind them for that structure of core ideas he believed was at the root of all diverse philosophies and religious experiences. He was not a man of such open mind that he had no convictions or commitments, but he refused to limit his vision to the "accepted," whether that meant the rigidity of official orthodox positions or the battle cries of the more vocal reformers.

Erasmus was not part of the power structures, neither a practicing cleric nor a government functionary. He was in fact a symbol for a whole new class in the struggle between Church and State: the literate, middle-class lay person whose loyalty had now to be courted by the official Church, the official State, and the Protestants. He was not powerful in that sense, but, as the most learned man of his time and its best-selling author, neither was he one of the powerless urban poor and peasant majority of the Church who could be coerced or led. Erasmus was like educated people who now make up a significant segment of the American Church today. But when Church reform became either/or, win/lose, choosing "sides," Erasmus rejected both coercion and simplism, since he placed truth above loyalty to a cause, and thus both sides ultimately rejected him as irresolute and spineless.

Erasmus did in fact stand for many propositions. (1) He was not anticlerical (against having priests) but anti-clericalism (against the clergy having the last-and-only significant word in any Church question). Literacy is power. For centuries clerics held a monopoly on literacy, but now many laymen were not only literate but also educators in schools and universities. What's more, for centuries "literacy" had meant fluency in Latin and Greek, but now translations and the printing press had begun to erode that barrier, too. There were now only two basic differences between most clerics and most literate laymen: ordination and celibacy. But neither ordination nor celibacy has anything to do with thinking out complex issues: in theology, law, morality, or Church reform.

On one hand, faith yields to the proposition that a priest can validly offer Mass and absolution, even if he is illiterate and a sinner. On the other, faith is strained to accept the proposition that a man can discover truth or come to a decision more surely if he is ordained to confer the sacraments or refrains from sexual intercourse — especially at a time when many decision-makers in the Church were not ordained and of those who were, many could not quite qualify as celibate.

(2) Erasmus proposed to make the scriptures available to as many

people as possible. This, of course, was now possible as never before because of the providential (and mixed) gift of the printing press. Jesus, after all, was not afraid to offer his message directly to an audience of ordinary people, without an interpreter, even though many would miss or garble his point, as the Apostles so consistently did. But for centuries the official Church had kept the scripture away from ordinary, even literate people who might "get ideas." Even after the long-delayed Council of Trent, that "protection" of the gospels from the people for whom they were written continued into the twentieth century.

(3) Erasmus argued for pluralism, tolerance of ideas that seem totally different from one's own, so that, sooner or later, a dialogue could show both "sides" where they were in agreement about the core of Christian truth, where they were actually saying the same things, only in different, apparently contradictory terms, and finally where their real differences lay — perhaps not over dedication to Christ, on either side, but on hidden agendas having more to do with power than with truth.

(4) Erasmus was quite definitely against what might be called "knee-jerk" Christianity, the surface, automatic, mechanical practice of a "faith" that has less to do with authentic symbols than with superstition, a belief that the symbols that focus faith have become themselves objects of faith, somehow "empowered" — like voodoo charms: relics, shrines, indulgences, Masses for the dead, as if one could manipulate God's will with incantations, purchase approval with good works, and "buy" salvation with "merit badges." Instead, he wanted to teach the faithful methods of genuine prayer, to open themselves to the movements of God, rather than trying to move God.

(5) Erasmus held for an absolute minimum of theology, not only about God but about human morality. No Christian, especially no child, needs or is capable of digesting the thoroughgoing, encyclopedic catechism that gives an answer for every conceivable question. It was precisely that mind-set that had gotten the Church in trouble for its twelve-hundred-year history. "Is it not possible," Erasmus wrote, "to have a fellowship with the Father, Son, and Holy Spirit, without being able to explain philosophically the distinction between them?"

But those moderate positions couldn't help but antagonize the "official Church": the theologians, canon lawyers, and decision-makers. After all, that's what the official Church had spent most of her official life trying to do: untangle all problems and put out the solutions in cookie-cutter clarity. She had discovered the phrase "one in being with the Father," which had separated her from the Arians, and the "Filioque," which had cut off the entire Eastern Church from Cairo to Moscow. What was constantly dividing the Church from itself was a compulsion to achieve a clarity and certitude of which no fallible human mind, or collection of them, is capable, especially when speaking of a God whose Mind infinitely escapes our categories.

A case in point occurred long after the break in the Church, when Protestantism itself was already breaking up into dissident sects. Lutherans held, with the Catholics, for transubstantiation in the Eucharist: that Jesus was physically present "in, with, and under" the bread and wine; Zwingli and his followers believed the bread and wine were merely symbols, no more "powerful" than a country's flag or a saint's statue; Calvinists held an unclear position somewhere between the two. The German Emperor, Charles V, a literate layman, struggled to get the four parties at least to agree that, *somehow*, "Christ is really and truly present in the Eucharist." In vain. "Somehow" was not good enough. And so, again, the Body of Christ was torn apart in the name of an unachievable uniformity.

Basically, Erasmus was asking the official Church to educate lay people in fundamental principles and then to trust them, to let them "grow up" as Christians, so that she wouldn't have to tell them down to the minutest detail what they could rightly do in their board rooms and bedrooms. If the Church wanted a moral laity with an inner grasp and commitment to the Spirit of Christ, rather than mere outward conformity, the answer was not to come from the theologian, nor from the canonical legalist, nor from the Inquisitor. That could come only from the educator who taught them to read and to think, and from the well-read, compassionate priest with whom they could honestly critique their own ideas. But as yet there were still not even any real seminaries for parish priests. Luther himself, an Augustinian, had been ordained at the age of twenty-four after only two years' training.

Originally, Erasmus found no real difficulty in Luther's "Ninety-five Theses." Later, however, when Luther began to invoke the power of the German princes to impose his vision of Christianity on their people, Erasmus was disillusioned in him and referred to him privately as a "Goth," a man of the brutal past. The question was no longer a matter of truth but a matter of power. Luther called all true Christians to "wash your hands in the blood of cardinals, popes, and other dregs of the Roman Sodom"; and the Catholic theologians of Louvain spoke no less feelingly about Luther, calling for the death of "that pestilential fart of Satan whose stench reaches heaven." Erasmus pleaded with both sides for moderation, concessions, brotherhood. Again, in vain.

Martin Luther (1483–1546) was an ordained Augustinian monk

who, two years after his ordination, went through an agony of scruples over his inability to avoid sin. (Like Augustine, Luther was at least a crypto-Manichean, believing flesh is by its nature evil.) Suddenly, he was struck with the insight that would change his life — and the history of Europe: human beings cannot *help* being sinners. Original sin left us so totally corrupted that we are incapable of genuinely good works; everything we do — even our acts of virtue and generosity — is performed by beings God now finds as disgusting as dung. Thus, all our Pelagian efforts to redeem ourselves in God's eyes are useless.

And yet God's justice demands restitution, not only for the original sin but for each of our own personal sins. But that no longer matters! Jesus has done that for us. His death and resurrection could not change our unchangeably corrupt nature (we still go on sinning), but instead, in the case of the saved, Christ's merits cover the dunghill of their wickedness so that God no longer adverts to it. No victim of original sin and perpetrator of personal sin can merit that forgiveness, nor do we have to. We merely *accept* Christ's gift of forgiveness solely on *faith*. All we need is the *confidence* that we are indeed saved.

The true Church, then, is invisible, and all outward trappings merely external symbols: sacraments, the clergy, personal penance — the whole physical body of the institutional Church. (As we have seen, however, Luther still clung to the actual presence of Christ in the Eucharist: "I would rather drink blood with the papists than drink wine with the Zwinglians.")

Theoretically, Catholics like Erasmus, and even some clerics, did not have much quarrel with that, or with Luther's disciplinary ideas such as married clergy or vernacular scriptures and liturgies. But the matter was not merely theoretical. Nor was Luther merely a theoretician. Luther was a *force*.

Luther was far more a man of the common people than were the popes or emperors, theologians or canon lawyers, even than the lay humanists. He was not by any means an expert theologian, but he was a man of burning, evangelical passion — not merely against such disciplinary abuses as selling indulgences but against theological abuses like the Pelagian ideas about meriting God's forgiveness and approval by our good works. He was a tireless man, turning out at least one book every two weeks. And he was single-minded, which as we have seen is always fatal.

Luther began preaching tolerance; he found a profound response from the common people. Like most such men in history, he merely found which way the parade was heading and got in front of it. But the common folk found these new ideas a promise of release from their feudal enslavement both to Church and State. This man promised them they could indeed think for themselves, which both Church and State found far too dangerous — for the people's own good. When the common folk began rising up against their oppressors, Luther, as a matter not of truth but of overall strategy, threw himself on the side of the territorial princes: he needed them. Thus the German Empire split into a checkerboard of Catholic dukedoms and Protestant dukedoms, a phenomenon that would soon spread all over Europe.

Emperor Charles V, who was at the moment also desperately trying to hold back an invasion by the Turks in the East, wanted a general council to resolve the divisions in his empire. But the German princes themselves — and France, never a friend to anything German — wanted with equal vigor to keep Germany divided and preserve their own power, and they therefore put all their combined efforts into preventing a council, or at least delaying it. They succeeded for twenty-five years. Again, Church and Caesar.

The delay in calling a council was itself a factor in further delay. The longer the Church waited, the more the reformers themselves began to split up into differing factions, so that (as with the Arab world today) it was difficult for anyone seeking peace to know with whom to deal.

John Calvin (1509–64) was a French convert to Lutheranism who had sought refuge in Switzerland. A stern man, Calvin pushed Luther's doctrine to its extreme conclusion. With original sin, human beings became totally corrupt, but God, with total knowledge, knew from that moment which ones would be saved (the elect) and which ones would be damned (the majority). All human beings are "predestined." But why would a good God do something so cruel? Calvin's simple reply: "Because it pleases him to." How can you tell whether you are among the elect or the damned? Simply because you are an upright member of the Church. Even more simply put: As long as you are not excommunicated, you are safe.

Calvin set up a theocracy: the town councils were the elders of the Church; pastors made yearly inspection tours of every home to see if everything was "in order." It was such a Calvinist theocracy that the Pilgrims first set up in New England.

During the delay before the ecumenical council, in areas where either papists or dissenters were in a minority, they pleaded for tolerance; when either side made up the majority, they ruthlessly persecuted the others for their false beliefs. But, many felt, religion had always been so much a part of the fabric of the State that it could no more operate with two religions than it could operate with two different codes of law. Finally, in 1555, at least the civil side of the question was settled in the Peace of Augsburg, which declared that each prince would determine the religion of his territory: *cuius regio, ejus religio* ("whoever's territory, his religion"). If a prince converted to the opposite side, his subjects were back to the old tribal conversions going back to Constantine.

The revolt in England was quite different. The issues dividing the Church on the continent were over both doctrine and discipline, theology and practice. But in England, the issues were almost solely disciplinary and practical — one reason Roman Catholicism and Anglicanism are still so similar. Henry VIII had not only been an orthodox Catholic who had written a book against Luther, but after the break remained fairly orthodox by Roman standards and continued to be an enemy of Luther and Calvin.

Henry's principal reason for the break was that he needed a male heir, and his wife was apparently incapable of giving him one. After the break from Rome, the Church over which Henry assumed headship made some disciplinary changes: the Mass in English, dispensation from celibacy, confiscation of monasteries and convents (and their assets). But the point at issue was loyalty to the pope — despite his corruption or his sanctity — as having "the final word" because of his connection to St. Peter.

All subjects were required to swear an oath of allegiance to the English king as head of the Church in England. A relatively few chose imprisonment and execution rather than swear: Thomas More, John Fisher, Carthusian monks, and others. But most of the English — noble and peasant, literate and illiterate — found themselves, like the Duke of Norfolk in Robert Bolt's *A Man for All Seasons,* wondering what all the fuss was about. Their daily lives were hardly changed by having the king and his counsellors decide questions of theology and practice rather than a faraway pope — who also was the recipient of a second set of their taxes. Most of the bishops and clergy, including many order priests and nuns, left their celibacy behind without much lamentation. When Thomas Cromwell's spies roamed the country in search of dissent, their reports were disappointingly meager.

Within forty years of Luther's nailing up his theses, Catholics controlled Spain, Italy, Ireland, Poland, Southern Germany, and Latin America. France and the Netherlands were torn between both views. And the rest of the ever-expanding known world was Protestant.

Finally, the Council of Trent began in 1545 and continued off and on for the next eighteen years. The bishops and their attendant theologians debated the whole body of Christian doctrine and discipline in the light of the Protestant critique: scripture, original sin, justification by faith and good works, sacraments, especially baptism and confirmation, practical rules for teaching theology, preaching — all with threats and penalties. But no matter what its other values or flaws, the council demanded seminaries with strict standards before a man might be ordained and with strict monitoring from the man's bishop thereafter.

The twenty-five-year delay of the council and its eighteen-year duration were also providential in a way. During that time, reform-minded popes were able to assemble better staffs and began the first system of papal embassies in the world's capitals. They also encouraged the Franciscan reform, which resulted in the new Capuchin order and new communities of nuns like the Ursulines. And they also approved an order like none other before it, Ignatius Loyola's Society of Jesus.

Through Ignatius's month-long retreat, the Spiritual Exercises, candidates for the Society (as well as lay men and women) were offered the chance to see themselves in relationship to God as objectively as they possibly could: a grasp of the true nature of God and each of his creatures, which gave the retreatant the *freedom* to choose the truth. Then the retreatant made a life choice — based not on what was most personally appealing but based on which alternative would be "for the *greater* glory of God." Once that commitment had been made, once the essentials had been grasped, everything else was, at least in some degree, adaptable.

Men who chose to be Jesuits were to be more than merely literate, and the training time for Jesuit seminarians was twice as long as for diocesan priests: fifteen years. That long period was intended not only to make Jesuits learned but to subject them to a rigid discipline. Further, the long training was also interspersed by work with the destitute, so that the trainee would always know to whom he was being sent and so that his extensive learning did not make him arrogant. Because of their education, experience, and adaptability, Jesuits became known as "men of the world," often to their peril.

But if the Jesuits could educate themselves, surely they could educate others. Where the Inquisition (which wasted little love on the Jesuits) had formerly moved into trouble spots to uproot dissent by force, now a group of Jesuit teachers moved into areas where there was a chance to influence young men — and their parents and rulers — away from the ideas of the dissidents. Twenty-five years after the founding of the Society, at the time of its founder's death, there were a thousand Jesuits in over a hundred schools. In 1552, they founded a college in Rome to train German priests to return to their divided homeland. What's more,

Jesuits were soon popping up all over the globe in missions from Japan and China and India to South America.

The short reign of Pope Paul IV (1555–59) has to have been one of the most intense in the history of the Church. In four years, although he was seventy-nine when he began his reign, Paul IV drove paganism from the papacy for good. Whatever the faults of Paul's successors, and they have been many, they all have lived primarily as *priests*. Paul declared there were "enough laws already," and instead of enacting new laws sent out orders for the observance of the already existing ones.

There would be no dispensations for overly young candidates for bishop; trusted bishops were sent out to reform monasteries and convents (usually with a Jesuit in tow); and lists of possible new bishops were scrupulously sifted. Any priest or monk who had left his monastery to take civil employment was deprived of any income or educational degrees he had formerly enjoyed despite his absence. Bishops who held jurisdiction in more than one place (and the attached stipends) were ordered to restrict themselves to one diocese and reside in it. And every bishop was to begin building a seminary and have it ready for inspection.

Paul IV abolished the entire system of obligatory fees for those being considered for any office in the Church. By one stroke of the pen, he deprived himself of two-thirds of his revenues — which did not stop him for an instant.

He told the cardinals who had just elected him that he trusted none of them. He gave those who were not ordained three months to receive orders or resign. He demanded lists of their stipend-bearing offices, ordered them to choose one, and took the rest. In his new appointments, he paid not the slightest attention at all to the wishes of the emperors or kings or princes. And, fortunately, his successors followed his policies.

There was hope again.

~ Questions for Discussion ~

1. The chapter makes an argument for pluralism — the mutual tolerance of disagreeing ideas, that we have in most of the world today. But how practical is that in the real world? Does it work in Northern Ireland, Central America, the Arab states, southeast Asia? Why *doesn't* it work in those places? What are the real factors that at least seem to make pluralism a pipe dream? On the other hand, where does pluralism work, at least fairly well? And what are the factors that enable it to work?

2. Think back to the questions in Chapter 5: What would a prophet with the mind of God call to our attention rather sternly about the Church today — its leadership, its intellectuals, its ordinary membership, and its present dealings with governments, that is, the Church's present use of its various forms of power. Now reread the segment above about Erasmus. What would Erasmus say to today's Church if he came back for a visit? Don't just go for the easy stuff like, "Priests ought to be married." What would Erasmus say about your parish? Your school?

Chapter 11

Who's Got the "Right" Christianity?

THERE IS A DIFFERENCE between *heresy* and *schism.* Heresy denies an essential of the core message of Jesus Christ; if you were to deny either the divinity or the humanity of Christ, as the Adoptionists, Arians, and others did, you could quite possibly be a saint, but not an authentic Christian — any more than you could be a billionaire and an authentic Communist.

Schism is a splitting; it comes from the same Greek root as "schizophrenic," a split personality; something that should be energized by a single governing soul or spirit instead now has more than one soul. In the early Church, the great argument was whether Christianity itself was merely the extension and fulfillment of genuine Judaism, or whether it was in fact a schism from Judaism, and the Church decided it was the latter.

As we saw, there have been three major schisms within the Christian Church since the age of the major heresies: Eastern Orthodoxy, Protestantism, and Anglicanism, each of which is a sort of umbrella term for several or many independent sub-sects. The reason for their split from the larger Church body may not have been over an essential. All three, for instance, broke off from the larger segment of Christianity over the ultimate supremacy of the pope: that he had "the last word." Surely no member of those three Churches holds the primacy of the pope an essential of Christ's myth; otherwise they'd be Roman Catholics. In fact, each Church believes its breakaway was not a schism, like the Church's departure from Judaism, but rather the genuine "Remnant" separating itself from the corrupt majority, like the journey of Noah away from a degenerate people to begin afresh.

Until Vatican II, Roman Catholics referred to themselves somewhat triumphantly as "the one true Church" and to the other Christian Churches quite condescendingly as "heretics," often with a sizzling adjective attached in case anyone missed the point. Since that great coming-to-our-senses, however, the official Church carefully refers to all our fellow Christians as "our separated brethren." Any time we are more aware of what unites us than of what divides us, we're coming closer to what Christ intended us to be: "catholic," with open arms.

Each of the Christian Churches embodies the intentions of its common Founder. They all publicly worship God in and through Jesus Christ; they all accept the same myth, the same scriptures. Their members all try to live upright lives; they all try to serve their neighbor and to live lives of Christian forgiveness. None of them is perfect, but they all try.

There is a unity of baptism; each accepts the Christianity of a newcomer who has been baptized in another branch. Although there are doctrinal differences, all four communions hold more or less with the Apostles' Creed and with the decisions of the early Church General Councils, up until (but not after) the withdrawal of the Orthodox in 1054 A.D.

Many of the divisive doctrinal issues seem mere quibbling to anyone but a professional theologian. There were disputes between some of the dissident Churches and Roman Catholicism over the danger of exaggerating the role of Mary, but some Anglicans reverence her more than most Catholics. Not too many Christians — in any of the four main branches — are even aware of terms like "Filioque." And anyone who knows even as little Church history as this book has provided knows many of the disputes were so heavily influenced by powerful and self-serving personalities and by political, economic, and nationalist self-interests, that it is difficult to suppress the suspicion that the doctrine in dispute at the time was not the real issue on the table at all, like two parents fighting one another and using their child as a weapon. Surely the war in Northern Ireland today has nothing whatever to do with whether the pope is the vicar of Christ.

The three non-Roman communions differ most strongly with Roman Catholicism over the position and authority of the pope. Beyond that, one can say — again in the broadest terms — that the Orthodox are the most "churchy," in the sense of having a firm but flexible structure and a complex, highly symbolic, and long liturgy; the Protestants have very little structure and very little symbolism; the Anglicans embrace high, low, and middle, rooted in the rigid caste system in Britain, but also admitting that not everyone has the same tastes in styles of worship.

The Orthodox are mysterious, mystical, unwilling to adapt very much. In contrast, most classical Protestant churches stress the preaching of the sermon over liturgical rites, are down to earth rather than mystical, and are perhaps overly adaptable; some forms of Protestantism believe in the real presence of Christ within the bread and wine, some believe they are mere symbolic reminders, and some have no bread and wine at all. The Anglicans range from a "High" church more formal even than Roman Catholicism, through various "Middle" forms, to a "Low" church almost indistinguishable from fundamentalist Protestantism.

As with the world religions we considered in Chapter 4, I can critique the three non-Roman Christianities only from my own quite limited and fallible point of view — limited not because I am a closed-minded Roman Catholic, but because I am the person my experiences of life have made me, *one* of which was that I was a born-Catholic. The preceding chapters give ample evidence that I am not above criticizing Roman Catholicism as well. The convictions I brought to bear on that critique will be the same convictions with which I attempt to critique the sisters of Roman Catholicism. I will try to evaluate them with the same equity as Erasmus might have, if not with his eloquence and elegance.

As you read through, bracket off in the margins what you personally like about each version of the Christian myth.

The Orthodox

The very name "Orthodox" ("right belief") indicates that its members believe they are not just a new fruit dropped from an old tree — a schism — but rather the original tree itself, pruned of Roman falsehoods. They acknowledge the need for administrators in the Church: bishops, metropolitans (archbishops), and a patriarch, but the patriarch is simply "first among equals" with his bishops, and each of the patriarchates (divided by language and geography) is independent of the others. The patriarch of Constantinople has a symbolic priority because of his connection with the center of the former Eastern Empire but no authority over the others; he is by no means an Eastern Orthodox "pope." There are, in effect, fifteen different Orthodox Churches, and only an ecumenical council can propose new interpretations of doctrine. Even then, the whole membership must "experience" the new interpretation before it is valid. The Spirit is in the membership as a whole, not only in a leader or group of leaders.

Their doctrinal differences with the Roman Church, as we have seen, are primarily due to a different point of view, emphasizing the majesty and mystery of the Christian God rather than his humanity. Their only declaration about Mary is that she is the Mother of both God and man in Jesus, but they resent the definitions of the Immaculate Conception and the Assumption — not because they don't believe them true, but because the pope of Rome defined them rather than an ecumenical council.

All the Orthodox Churches hold the same seven sacraments as the Roman Church, but their Eucharistic liturgy is much more lush and majestic than the Roman rite. The clergy are clothed in heavy, gilded vestments, with high golden crowns; there is a great deal of choral singing and incense. The consecration itself takes place out of sight of the people in the pews, behind a wall of icons, and the whole rite lasts two hours or more.

Roman Catholicism recognizes the valid ordination of Orthodox priests. That is, it acknowledges their clergy are genuinely empowered to perform sacramental activities, ordained by bishops who themselves can trace an unbroken connection back to the Apostles who had been ordained by Jesus himself. The principal obstacle to reunion is the authority of the pope.

Orthodoxy is impressive. It is surely holy and, by Rome's own admission, traces its authority and sacramental power back to the Apostles. Orthodoxy appeals to me because it is more "democratic," which is the result of my being American. But to my mind it is not "catholic," since it is restricted more or less by national and geographic separatism. Nor is it unified in any more than a surface sense, a symbolic union that has no substance beneath the symbolism.

The Church Jesus founded was intended, quite clearly, to reach out as far as possible, "to the ends of the earth," and to embrace men and women of all shades of political attitude, race, language, social position, color. To unite that transcultural entity, as with any society, there has to be a single director, perhaps less firm and more flexible than many popes have been, but someone more than a mere symbol, like the Queen of England.

Finally, on a completely personal bias, although I admit a nostalgia for the majesty of the pre–Vatican II Mass, I must confess that a well-prepared half-hour liturgy serves my soul's needs more than a two-hour liturgy, no matter how majestic. And I've forgotten all my Greek, and the Slavic languages are as meaningless to me as Mandarin.

Protestants

The reforms of the first Protestant, Martin Luther, were intended at first to force the Church to forget the encrustations of tradition and return to the gospel, to rip away the time-conditioned and humanly inspired changes, to get rid of all the head-trip, left-brain, knee-jerk posturings and return to simplicity, surrendering to the forgiving power of the God Who Made Us. It was not merely the unworthiness of so many of the

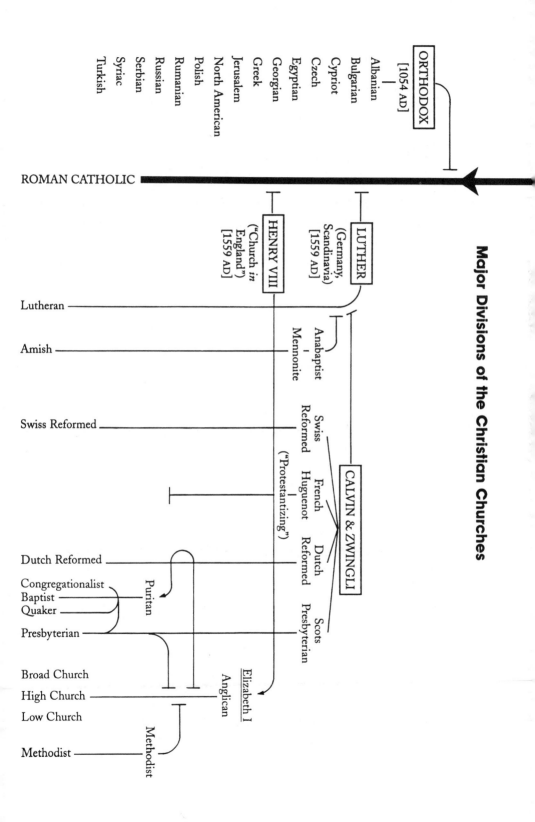

Major Divisions of the Christian Churches

ORTHODOX [1054 AD]

Albanian
Bulgarian
Cypriot
Czech
Egyptian
Georgian
Greek
Jerusalem
North American
Polish
Rumanian
Russian
Serbian
Syriac
Turkish

ROMAN CATHOLIC

LUTHER (Germany, Scandinavia) [1559 AD]

HENRY VIII ("Church in England") [1559 AD]

CALVIN & ZWINGLI

Elizabeth I

Lutheran

Amish

Anabaptist – Mennonite

Swiss Reformed

Swiss Reformed

French Huguenot

Dutch Reformed

Scots Presbyterian

("Protestantizing")

Dutch Reformed

Congregationalist
Baptist
Quaker

Puritan

Presbyterian

Broad Church

High Church

Low Church

Anglican

Methodist

Methodist

clergy — including so many popes — that incensed him; it was also the official Church's clinging to the pseudo-importance of externals rather than to the Spirit who animates the Body of Christ. But Luther was not merely a "naked mind" himself; he was an impassioned man who often lost his balance.

Jesus had thundered against the legalistic leadership of the Jewish religion from which he ultimately removed his people. Paul, the former Pharisee, had rejected the Law and its endless formulas and practices that "insured" salvation and "bribed" God's favor. It was precisely those legalistic, superstitious, and non-essential questions Luther believed had drawn the Church's attention away from the fundamental message of Christ.

What's more, the whole system of relics, indulgences, and stipend Masses not only was a kind of clerical embezzlement but also was superstitious, a form of Pelagianism institutionalized by the very Church that had condemned Pelagianism. Christians cannot "buy" God's approval; they can only *accept* it.

Therefore, Luther rejected a privileged clergy — privileged not only in terms of worldly power but in terms of spiritual power — and preached the "priesthood of all believers." Of course, by rejecting a central authority, he also rejected anything but the remotest sense of unity among Protestants. In struggling for the values of independence, he sacrificed the values of bonding.

Further, he wanted to free the faithful from exaggerated ritual pomp (much as the reforms after Vatican II did). The hoopla of a majestic liturgy became no more than a "show," to which one could respond thrillingly, even as an atheist. For the intellectuals, it was merely a theatrical experience; for the unschooled, it was nothing more than voodoo superstition. So he stripped the liturgy of all gaudy vestments and "sacred" symbols. All those were crutches, substitutes for authentic faith in the saving Christ. But Luther, man of the ordinary people, forgot something very important about ordinary people: The majority of them don't have that kind of faith. Their faith is weak: "Lord, I believe. Help my unbelief!" The ordinary folk need crutches.

What's more, in the Lutheran view, one "puts on Christ" as he or she might put on a garment, to "fool" God about the sinner still inside the deceptive garment. Thus, at one and the same time, the elect are righteous (because of Jesus) and yet also detestable (because of original sin and their own sins). I just find it difficult to accept a God that easily deceived, a God that dumb. I find it even more difficult to accept a God who could nurse a grudge, with no possibility of forgiveness, from the beginning of humankind until forever — and tell me through Jesus Christ that I, a sinner, should nonetheless forgive my brother or sister "seventy times seven times." To my fallible mind, the God of Martin Luther and his followers has no relation whatever with the all-forgiving father of the Prodigal Son.

Because of Luther's stress on the independent soul, the divisions and subdivisions of evangelical (scripture only) Protestantism are almost innumerable.

Lutherans are highly evangelical, that is, they stress the superiority of the scriptures over any "official" interpretations. The individual is empowered — without intrusion by any clerical priesthood, or theologians, or traditions — to discern the meaning the scriptures offer him or her. But, again to my mind, to believe that any individual, schooled or unschooled, could interpret what Jesus said — from within an Aramaic mind-set, which was then translated by a Greek mind-set, and then translated by an English mind-set — without any interference from linguistic experts seems to require a miraculous intervention by God in each individual case, as powerful as God's inspiration of the biblical prophets. When I hear how badly born-again Christians can mangle the scriptures, my faith in such inspiration suffers a test it cannot rise to.

The only two sacraments the Lutherans retain are baptism and the Lord's Supper, which, depending on the sect, may actually be the Body and Blood of Christ or merely symbols. The question of the Real Presence is something far too complex to deal with here. I've believed all my life that Jesus is, as the Emperor Charles V said, *somehow,* "there." But if you asked me to "prove" that, I could no more succeed than I could "prove" that my friends love me. There's too much right-brain in there to admit of a left-brain "proof."

Calvinists (any Church with "Reformed" in its title) broke from Lutheranism principally because Lutheranism wasn't as tough as reality demanded. Human beings are even worse than Luther dared to say they are. And although Calvinists acknowledge no single central authority like the pope, the elders are elected in service to the community: to see that they don't mess up. There is more than a little similarity between classical Calvinism and the totalitarian "informant" states of Nazi Germany and Stalinist Russia. There is also a similarity to the mind-set of the Inquisition. A Calvinist segment broken from Anglicanism landed at Plymouth Rock and later conducted the Salem witch trials.

Presbyterians, a development of Calvinism, maintain there is not only no need for a pope but no need for bishops to keep order and to ordain.

They are governed by elected elders and a system of courts. They also hold for only two sacraments: baptism and the Lord's Supper, which may be as elaborate or as spare as the particular community's tastes.

Congregationalists differ from other Protestants only in that each individual community is independent of all the others, though joined in a feeling of fellowship. These are, for the most part, descendants of the American Calvinist Puritans. There are no bishops or presbyters. Their more common name now is the United Church of Christ.

Baptists (who again have innumerable subdivisions) deny infant baptism and require that a person be baptized (usually by immersion) only after a free and adult commitment to Christ. Many are strict fundamentalists, holding every word of scripture literally true, for instance, the snake in the Genesis story actually, historically spoke to a woman named Eve. Their worship services are generally without bread and wine and allow for a great deal of enthusiastic participation from the congregation.

Methodists broke away from Anglicanism in favor of a more Calvinist view of Christianity, but, unlike Calvinists, they brought the office of bishop with them from Anglicanism. Their name comes from their methodical devotion to study and religious practice, and they believe one is "saved" not by good works but solely by faith in Jesus Christ. Like Calvinists, they are, at least in their classical form, strongly opposed to liquor, dancing, card-playing, and so forth.

Quakers (the Religious Society of Friends) lay special stress on inspiration by the Holy Spirit: the "Inward Light." They are strictly pacifist and have no formal rites or ministers. Instead they sit quietly in meditation, and if one of the members feels moved by the Inward Light, he or she speaks. They refuse to serve in the armed forces or to take an oath.

Mormons (the Church of Christ of Latter-day Saints) are a relatively recent American sect who see divine revelation coming not only through the Bible but also through the visions of their leaders, especially the vision of their founder, Joseph Smith, recorded in the *Book of Mormon.* They faithfully give one-tenth of their earnings to the Church and two years of service during which the member has no other job, and they can marry no one, without the approval of the elders — who frequently assign a spouse. If one chooses to marry a non-Mormon, either the non-Mormon must convert or the Mormon must leave the church. The leadership is a three-member First Presidency and a Council of Twelve (Apostles).

Jehovah's Witnesses believe the end of the world will come in their lifetime. They, too, are sternly pacifist and refuse to salute the flag or bear arms or participate in government. All members are considered ministers, and they engage in vigorous door-to-door recruitment, as do the Mormons.

Unitarians are not really Christian at all. They reject a Trinity in favor of a single divine Person, believing, as the Adoptionists, that Jesus was the greatest of moral teachers but not the embodiment of God. They hold no common profession of faith and have a kind of Congregationalist governance. They are staunchly devoted to issues of human dignity and rights.

No one could call Protestantism *a* Church. Rather it is a name given to those Christians who are not Roman Catholic or Orthodox or Anglican. Its members are as independent of one another as the members of the United Nations. The one authority in all Protestant subdivisions is the scriptures and, true to the principle of equality of all members, anybody's opinion is as good as anyone else's. They stress the priesthood of all believers, though lay people are generally not allowed to preach, and ministers are ordained by other ministers.

The great Protestant theologian Paul Tillich called this moment in history "the end of the Protestant era," implying most Protestant churches are likely to be absorbed into others. Liberal Protestants' attempt to demythologize scripture, to remove the symbolic and mysterious from it, has had a strong effect on intellectual Anglicans and Roman Catholics; biblical scholars accept one another's insights across sectarian lines. Vatican II incorporated into Roman Catholicism a great many of the changes Luther called for, especially regarding involvement of the laity and the legitimacy of at least a kind of pluralism.

My own reasons for choosing a myth-system other than the Protestant one are expressed in a statement of the eminent Protestant theologian Karl Barth:

> At those times when the task of being ministers of the divine word, as we of the Reformed Churches say, has worried and oppressed us, have we not all felt a yearning for the rich services of Catholicism, and for the enviable role of the priest at the altar? When he elevates the *Sanctissimum*, with its full measure of that meaning and power which is enjoyed by the *material* symbol over the symbol of the human word as such [a real sacrifice rather than merely a sermon], the double grace of the sacrificial death and the incarnation of the Son of God is not only preached in words but actually takes place in his hands, and the priest becomes "creator of the Creator" before the people. Even at the mass the Bible is displayed, but how unimportant, how indifferent a matter is the

delivery of the sermon based on it. And yet again, how completely the poorest of sermonettes is transfigured by the saving radiance of the eucharistic miracle!

Protestants are quite obviously holy and surely "catholic," since they welcome all people, despite even their theological differences. But, as Barth says, their ritual does not even claim to transform. And they are quite clearly not united.

Finally, the scriptures were written in Hebrew and Greek, then translated into English. Even if you took only two or three different English translations and compared them word by word, you would see a wide range of differences. Which translation is closest to the original intentions of the writers? In the case of the gospels, how much have the personal biases of the four evangelists skewed the original intention of Jesus? To say that God "stepped in" and whispered what he wanted to say in each of their ears is too simplistic.

To say anybody off the street could interpret something as complex — and important — as the scriptures is equivalent to saying anybody off the street could read and understand Shakespeare or Freud. Jesus did speak to all men and women, of all ages and cultures, but he had to use words and symbols meaningful in a *particular* age and culture. Few ordinary folk would pick up Plato (who also spoke to all ages, but from within a particular language and culture) and expect to understand him without help. Why should the scriptures be different?

Anglicans

The beginning of Anglicanism as a separate Christian Church occurred, as everyone admits, for purely political rather than religious reasons: Henry VIII wanted an heir to succeed him. Thus, the main objection of Anglicanism to Roman Catholicism is the authority of the pope. At present, Anglicans have also shown themselves more liberal in disciplinary questions such as divorce, birth control, and ordination of women.

Anglicans do not consider themselves "Protestants" at all, but rather "Anglo-Catholics." They are called "Episcopal" because they have bishops who are empowered by ordination and who at least "guide" the minds of the faithful. The High Church has a liturgy all but indistinguishable from the Roman Catholic rite; the Broad Church has a "Communion Service" and is given more to hard-nosed rationalism than to symbolism; the Low Church may or may not have a Communion Service and is distinctly evangelical, leaning toward feelings more than to rational doctrines.

Like the other two non-Roman communions, much of Anglican unity is founded on common interest — or common disagreements from other groups — about the power of the clergy and the strictness of morality. The Lambeth Conference of Anglican Bishops has no binding force on any Anglican; it is merely suggestive. The bishops are not the authentic interpreters of scripture, nor do they offer anything more than moral guidelines. Rather they are the agency by which authentic ordination is handed on.

Pope Leo XIII's denial of the validity of Anglican ordination delivered a severe blow to the possibility of reunion. In regard to the importance of Anglicanism to its membership: In 1958, of the 27 million Anglicans worldwide, only two million received Communion on Easter Sunday.

Anglicanism is appealing because of its compassion on such issues as divorce, birth control, homosexuality, and the ordination of women. I have been to their liturgies, and they reminded me of the Roman ritual when I was young. Its members, as in all the other communions, are holy or try to be. Despite Leo XIII's denial, the validity of their ordination seems, at least to me, a technicality any pope could reverse. But something in my personal make-up likes things "neat and focused" — not the finicky, nit-picking of doctrines till one has "certitude," but a sense of organic "wholeness" to the Christian community.

I have disagreed — perhaps too strongly and too often — with many of the pronouncements (or lack of them) from the six popes under whom I've lived. Once I have reasoned out the grounds for my differences as well as I can, I have led my life accordingly, not in defiance of the pope but in "loyal opposition," ready to face the God I know through Jesus Christ if I've judged wrongly.

But no matter what my differences, the pope is a force in my life. In a world of materialism, exploitation, capitalistic or communistic saber-rattling, and nationalist divisions, there is always a focal, powerful figure who comes forward to remind us what we are: human beings, whose common humanity far outweighs the causes of our squabbles. Especially in a world that has shrunk to a "Global Village," there has to be a powerful voice for reason. And, realistically, that is not going to be the patriarch of Constantinople or the archbishop of Canterbury.

The pope is for me, in a word, a father. I don't always agree with my father. But I need one.

The history of the Roman Church shows a kind of unnatural life, nearly miraculous, working in what so often should have been a corpse. It "should" have died in the Roman arenas. It should have died in the barbarian invasions, in the Arian heresy, in the split between East and West, in the Islamic conquest of half the known world, in the turbulence of the Reformation.

It should have died not only from those assaults from without, but also, so very often, from the corruption and stupidity within: the Inquisition, the Crusades, the witch hunts, the moral depravity of its leaders, the squabbles over minute doctrinal questions of no importance whatever to the ordinary believer. It should have died of sterility in the days of its arch-conservatism. It should have died before the onslaughts of the Enlightenment, of Scientism, of Materialism.

But the old chaste whore didn't.

~ Questions for Discussion ~

1. Most of us became Roman Catholic Christians through no choice of our own. Like our parents' convictions about toilet training, treatment of siblings, and "the important things in life," Catholicism was "taped" into our superegos before we were able to reason about it. Now we can. Brainstorm the elements Jesus would expect to find, if he came back on an inspection tour, in any community that used his name and claimed to embody his myth. Which of the four great Christian communions (despite unavoidable imperfections) seems most to embody that community.

2. Many non-Roman Christian communions emphasize "the priesthood of all believers" more than the Roman Church, with its long history of clerical dominance. The priesthood of all believers has a special appeal, especially to Americans who treasure democracy. Priests and bishops are ordained to administer the sacraments and monitor the "prophecies" of the community members. But priests and bishops are not the only ones with ideas, especially in a well-educated community. By your baptism, you were also "ordained" into the priesthood of believers and, as a Christian, you have a right to be heard. What's more, you have an *obligation* to be heard.

Make a list of the items you'd bring up if you had a no-holds-barred private meeting with the pope.

Now, what are you going to do with the list?

Chapter 12

The Modern and
Post-modern Church

FORTRESSES ARE REASSURING. They keep the enemy securely outside and the good guys securely inside. And we all want security. But fortresses are another mixed blessing — especially when a lot of those inside are really enemies in disguise, and when a lot of the "enemies" outside really have truth to share.

The Hebrews fell victim to a "fortress mentality," carefully guarding traditions within rigid walls of an unchallengeable Law, protecting it from the "contamination" of outside ideas. In a sense they made adherents of the Law believe changing times were an aberration to be shunned. But in walling off its myth from new — true — insights, Judaism was also "protecting" itself from evolution, which, judging from the nature of the Creator we see in the universe, was not quite what God had in mind.

Once the life-and-death struggles of the sixteenth-century schisms had settled and the bulwarks were rebuilt, the Catholic Church was again protected by walls that not only defended its unity but also repelled healthy cross-fertilizing by new and at first seemingly threatening ideas. In fact, for the first 1,950 years of the Church's history, "syncretism" was a word only one or two notches up the scale from "heresy." Such a fortress mentality was not only contradictory to the God who offers new evolutionary challenges through history, but also contradictory to the Jesus who sent the Church out to make his message understandable to all nations, all cultures, all times.

Two terms will recur in the following pages that need clarification from the outset: "Liberalism" and "Absolutism."

We all have a vague sense of what the term "Liberalism" means, as in, "Her parents are too liberal with her," too undemanding, too nonintrusive. As we saw before when speaking of the "Left" and the "Right," Liberalism is a relative term, covering a spectrum of convictions from anarchy and total rejection of any restriction at the extreme left, through

Communism, through support of welfare programs, to merely a desire that the poor and exploited get a fair shake. Then you get to the "Middle of the Road," when everything starts shading into Conservatism.

When the term "Liberal" occurs in history books, it often means any new movement that resents restriction — whether that be the restriction reason imposes on belief, or the restriction belief imposes on reason, or the restriction morality places on business and politics, or the restriction government puts on private property and affairs in the form of taxes, labor laws, and regulation of trade. In economics, liberals who resent government intrusion are called, paradoxically, conservatives.

"Absolutism," obviously, is not a relative term at all, as in "You're absolutely, totally, completely right!" Absolutists are not just right; they have the only admissible answer. To their own minds absolutists are not only right in the sense of "correct" but have the "right" to impose their views on others not equally clear-sighted. We have seen absolutism throughout history, on both sides of nearly every steamy issue, each side trying to make up in zeal and coercion for what it lacks in certitude — a triumphalism and totalitarianism that we will unfortunately see again and again, in both Church and State, and that will now also be carried like a banner by two new forces, money and mobs, as the human family evolves out of feudalism into the ages of capitalism and democracy; "certitudes" will erupt in revolutions that (for a time) tear the fabric of society apart.

Absolutism — claimed by Church, State, university, or common people — denies the need for balancing. Rather, it is a game, like Monopoly (as in "monopoly capitalism"): The object of the game is for only *one* player to win. And all other players lose.

Again, to my mind, the yearning for certitude *is* the original sin, of which all other sins are merely photocopies. In the Genesis myth, the prototype of all sins, Adam and Eve wanted to "become like God," to have all the answers: certitude. It was the yearning of Oedipus, Hamlet, Faust. It was the taproot of the early heresies, of the divisions of the Body of Christ into rival factions, and finally of the schism into four completely separated Christian Churches, each claiming to be the one true fortress — like kids who won't make up, pick up the ball, and go home to sulk, only on a global scale. Such a quest for absolutist certitude negates the whole lesson Jesus intended when he "emptied himself," becoming amnesiac about his divine certitude, so he could learn the only way a *human* can: step by step.

When the Church — or State, or university, or the common people — forget that lesson, convince themselves that they, and only they, have the certain truth that will "solve it all," a truth so airtight that it can be enriched neither by differing views nor by re-examination, we are back at the gates of Eden. Original sin: narcissism that refuses to admit one has made a mistake, plus inertia that says it would be too humiliating to admit one's mistake and go back to the first wrong turn.

The history of the People of God has always been and continues to be an endless recopying of the original mistake.

The Church and Reason: 1600–1700

The Treaty of Westphalia (1648), which ended the Thirty Years' War between France and Germany, essentially dictated the disposition of Church affairs in a ruined Germany and was conducted without any consultation with the reigning pope. It was the end of an epoch. The pope had become, simply, irrelevant. The participants were now "big boys" and had no need for a "Daddy" to solve Church problems for them. For nearly two hundred years the papacy ceased to have any significant influence on international affairs. Thus, for the first time since the catacombs, the secular State became almost indilutedly that: secular. With the rise of the merchant class, religion was fine for the women and children, but business is business.

The Age of Reason was not necessarily at odds with religion, yet. In England, reason and religion worked together like two placid oxen in the same yoke. In France, however, reason and religion came at one another like raging bulls.

In England, both Isaac Newton and Robert Boyle had no trouble discerning God through his work in nature; in fact the order and purpose scientists found in creation was the surest argument against atheism. Yet rationalist philosophers did not want a God too active in his creation; such a stress would lead to paganism, priests once again trying to manipulate the God within matter with relics and mumbo-jumbo — for a price.

One such was John Locke (1631–1704), as business-like a philosopher as you're likely to find, who tried to forge a union between Christian morality and the newly emerging capitalist system. No nonsense, no frills, no defining the Undefinable: just a good solid commercial contract between the individual and God. It was still quite clear there was a God; in Locke's time atheists were remarkably rare. As he said in his typical unemotional prose: "The human mind cannot be produced by a purely material cause. Hence the cause of our existence must be a cognitive being." Aside from that the number of doctrines should be pared to a bare minimum, since usually the minor issues "breed implacable enmity among Christian brethren, who are all agreed in the substantial and truly fundamental part of religion."

Christ didn't come to change how we think; he came to change how we act. He showed us that it was just good long-range business practice to keep our affairs with the Almighty in order; ethics and morality just didn't make any sense outside the economic metaphor of profit-and-loss: heaven or hell. In Locke's utilitarian Christianity, a person would have to be a proper fool not to live a moral life. Nor did Locke seem to be troubled by the fact that a Christianity that was, pure and simple, no more than "enlightened self-interest" directly contradicted the selflessness its Founder had intended at its core.

Along with Spain, France had always had a focal position in the Roman Church, since it was one of the few places in Europe not "Protestantized." Not for long. In *Augustinus,* Bishop Cornelius Jansen (1585–1638) ignited what became a new outbreak of an old heresy: Jansenism, a reworking of Manicheanism. It maintained everything purely natural is evil, and the human will is totally powerless against the evil temptations embedded within its own nature — except with an irresistible gift of grace, which God gives to very few. It begins to sound familiar: Jansen is "reading St. Augustine through John Calvin's spectacles," and what all three find there is a disgusting humanity: Manicheanism.

Before the Council of Trent, even Catholics who attended Mass weekly rarely received communion. But the council exhorted them to receive at every Mass they attended, and this practice was preached all over Europe and the missions. But Jansen and the gloomy elite of "super-Catholics" who followed him never had the ugliness of human nature too far from their minds. Without *absolutely* (note the word) *perfect* contrition, both the sacrament of penance and communion became *new* mortal sins. Since communion is a reward only for the most virtuous, denying oneself communion, as a penance, was proof of virtue. So it became a virtue not to receive! Jansen based this doctrine, ludicrously, on Jesus' statement: "Man does not live by bread alone."

It is difficult to believe such a wretched belief about humanity (and its Creator) could have spread so widely, and not only in France; it also proved (ferociously) appealing to the Irish, wherefrom it spread throughout America along with the immigrant Irish clergy. To see it at its worst, read the third chapter of James Joyce's *Portrait of the Artist as a Young Man.* There have been a rash of plays, novels, and films about the sin-conscious, hell-fire Church those over forty today were brought up in.

It's laughable now, to think we fell for it so unquestioningly. What is even more bewildering is that Jansenism appealed to so many geniuses as well — for three hundred years.

Blaise Pascal (1623–62) was a scientist-mathematician but also a profound essayist who fell almost eagerly into the dark quicksand of Jansenist pessimism. He stood for a separatist French Church and was "a Catholic Lutheran," basically against any organized religion at all. It is difficult to comprehend how a man who exercised reason so ingeniously in other fields should opt for a view of humankind that makes us guilty of sin simply by being born human, over which none of us had any control.

Still, it is possible to trace modern pessimism — expressed most eloquently in our own day by French atheist-existentialists like Jean Paul Sartre and Albert Camus — back through Pascal, to Jansen, to Augustine, to Tertullian, to Manicheanism.

The Church and Deism: 1700–1800

The Enlightenment was the first philosophical system evolved completely outside of the Church in over a millennium. Its practitioners were called *philosophes* who composed the first Encyclopedia, what all the best minds then knew about history, geography, and the whole human enterprise, all written with a subtle but distinctly anti-Catholic bias. In an age when to-be-civilized meant to-be-French, the Encyclopedia was read eagerly all over the world and became a kind of universal educator.

The *philosophes,* mostly Deists with a sprinkling of atheists, relied on pure reason, without recourse to any "revealed scriptures." Catholicism and even Christianity were a matter left to the unthinking masses. Many of them believed science and philosophy soon would provide humankind with a secular paradise: "the best of all possible worlds," a triumphal dream not without its adherents even today, who believe science will "solve all the problems." This is called "millenarianism," a belief that within a thousand years (a millennium), secular society, as a gradually purified reality, will replace the corrupt institutional myth of the Church. The Nazi "Thousand-Year Reich" and Communism are millenarian myths. So, at its birth, was Christianity.

To lay the rational foundations for this paradise obligated the Enlightenment to uproot completely all institutional religion, with its irrational superstitions and pig-headed, absolutist clergy. The Enlightenment would substitute a love of here-and-now humanity for love of the inaccessible and unknowable God.

The *philosophes* also had the secret brotherhood of Freemasons all over the world, to which many of the founding fathers of the United States and a majority of its presidents have belonged. In the secret symbols of the Masons — triangles, T-squares, and astrolabes — one can discern their roots in Voltaire's statement: "I believe in God, not the god of mystics and theologians, but the god of nature, the great geometrician, the prime mover, unalterable, transcendental, everlasting . . . who, by his nature and mine, must remain incomprehensible to me."

Voltaire (1694–1778) was the best known of the *philosophes:* essayist, dramatist, historian, and author of the novel *Candide,* the most relentless satire ever written against all organized religions, particularly Catholicism and Jesuits. This was not the frontal attack of the Jansenists; the Church could handle that. But how does one handle innuendo? Especially when it is very, very funny. But Voltaire's purpose was very, very serious. He wrote to Frederick the Great: "Your Majesty will do the human race an eternal service in uprooting this infamous superstition [the Church]. Not from among the rabble, who are not worthy of being enlightened and who are worthy of any yoke. I mean from among the well-bred, from among those who wish to think."

Voltaire also wrote to a friend, "When we have destroyed the Jesuits, we shall have easy work with the Infamy [the Church]."

First, the king of Portugal banned Jesuits in Europe and in their extensive missions in his South American and Asian colonies; France followed suit; finally, all the Bourbon kings prevailed on Pope Clement XIV in 1773 to suppress the Society throughout the world: 22,000 Jesuits from all over Europe and from 273 foreign missions were driven from their houses with nothing more than a cassock and a breviary. Paradoxically, only Frederick II of Prussia (a Protestant) and Catherine the Great of Russia (an Orthodox) refused to enact the decree of Jesuit suppression — from no great love for Catholicism but because the Jesuits were such good educators. For forty years, Jesuits lived a sort of shadow existence in eastern Europe. The effect of their withdrawal from the missions and from education was incalculable.

On July 14, 1789, the French revolutionaries stormed the Bastille to end the repression of the aristocracy and Church in France. Church property was confiscated and, by the end of 1789, all priests, nuns, and monks had been dispersed, just as the Jesuits had been. As in the days of Henry VIII, an oath regarding the supremacy of the State over the Church was required under pain of death. It was a revolution not unlike the later Communist revolutions in Russia and China: de-Christianization by guillotine. Some 30,000 to 40,000 priests who refused the oath became prisoners or exiles; between 2,000 and 5,000 were executed. About 20,000 of the priests who had sworn the oath agreed to be de-Christianized; 43 bishops gave up their rank, although only 23 actually rejected Christianity.

Most critical, Catholic universities were replaced by strictly secular institutions. Theology was banned. The seeds were sown for the present-day supermarket multiversity.

For two hundred years, France, "the eldest daughter of the Church," had resisted the replacement of Catholicism with Lutheranism; now within a few short years, France rejected not only Catholicism but Christianity with it, and in its place enshrined Deism.

But what could take the place of that emotional gap left by the uprooting of religion? The same thing that filled that gap when the Hebrews were surrounded by Canaanites, and the same thing that attempts to fill that gap today: *Party!*

After the revolution, "religion" became organized hedonism, liturgical debauchery. In August 1793, a pagan celebration took place around the statue of Nature erected at the Bastille, spurting water from her breasts. In November of that year, the Cathedral of Notre Dame was "reconsecrated" as the Temple of Reason, represented by a naked woman cavorting on the high altar. At times in these temples, physicians and scientists would act as priests, replacing the Mass with laboratory experiments.

It comes as no surprise that it didn't work. As P. T. Barnum, who was in essentially the same business, said later, "You can't fool all of the people all of the time." Obviously, Deism and rationalism alone tipped the balance too far. Without the right brain, the left brain goes haywire. Unbalanced rationalism was bound to fail in eighteenth-century France just as it has failed again in twentieth-century Russia and China. There was no place for genuine human — much less religious — emotion above the level of the genitals. The greatest gift the excesses of the French Revolution gave the Church was to make it look normal.

The Church and Liberalism—Against the Tide: 1800–1900

Three new factors now entered the geopolitical game: a reinvigorated papacy, the emergence of a rigorously left-brain scientific method that single-mindedly rejected the subjective for the purely objective, and a newly discovered power in the teeming millions of working people in the cities. It would be the age that generated Karl Marx. And Pope Leo XIII.

Rationalism began to "threaten" religion again with the publication of the theories of Charles Darwin (1731–1802), Sigmund Freud (1856–1939), and Friedrich Schleiermacher (1768–1864).

Darwin offered a view of the emergence of humans that directly contradicted Genesis, at least taken literally, as it had always been. Freud undermined the theory of human guilt; human beings are prisoners of their programming (the Superego) and of irrational subconscious urges (the Id), no more capable of genuine responsibility, and therefore guilt, than an animal. Schleiermacher, a liberal Protestant biblical scholar, showed scripture was a highly subjective collection, which furthermore consisted of layers upon layers of later additions. Without the Bible, and without the need for personal responsibility, Christianity seemed now to be of interest only to historians.

But accepting those new discoveries as true did not mean everything the Church (and the rest of the world) had accepted as true had suddenly become false. It meant only that all everyone had believed before that time was now shown to be *inadequate* to what the truth now showed itself to be.

Authentic truth is never a threat to authentic religion. These new discoveries meant merely that the Church had to go back and rethink her whole myth once again in new terms — just as she had to rethink when she cut herself off from Judaism and moved out into a Greek-thinking world, when the literal End of the World did not come, when she suddenly found herself married to the empire, when the empire collapsed and she found herself Cinderella again, when the unexpected discovery of the pagan Aristotle, the Far East, and the New World made her widen her horizons to what the possibilities of being human meant, when she'd risen from the ashes once again in the Renaissance and found she was a whore. Now the Church was in danger of discovering simple faith is not enough; faith is a calculated risk, and in order to make a genuine act of faith, she had to teach her members how to think.

At its deepest level, the very *purpose* of the official Church is continuously to rethink the Person and message of Jesus in the light of new discoveries and to retranslate that message (1) without violating Jesus' original intentions and yet (2) honestly accommodating whatever is true in these new discoveries and (3) explaining the final outcome in terms meaningful to the ever-revolving New People of God.

The whole process of being Christian is the experience of metanoia: *conversion,* not just once-for-all, but over and over, both in the official Church and in the individual Catholic. Conversion is painful, but struggle and rebirth are the gospel! Conversion flies directly in the face of the self-defensive narcissism and inertia that we have called original sin. It means opening your eyes to the truth, no matter how painful, and bowing to it.

But, for the next hundred years, that was precisely what the official, absolutist Church was too proud to do.

Ironically, some non-Catholics were responding to the new rationalist challenges in a way one might suspect an evolutionary Creator would want them to: They painfully re-examined both the new scientific insight and their own faith. This was true of the Anglican Oxford Movement, among whose members the most famous was John Henry Newman. Suddenly, rationalism — the primary intention of which was to free men and women from institutional religion and right-brain thinking — was driving men and women toward Rome. Rome suddenly appeared a fortress "amid the encircling gloom." In the democracies that had put down their roots in the previous century and the new ones gradually emerging, the ability to persuade large blocks of voters was now a new source of *power*, not only in the official Church but also in unions, ethnic groups, and so forth. "Catholic public opinion" now became important again, not just in the sense that the medieval popes had the power to control events by excommunicating kings, but that Catholic opinion in any country could now have the same significant effect on the outcome of an election of the new kind of ruler. And if the pope, bishops, and priests effectively "controlled" the consciences of Catholics, the Church could "deliver the votes" — or not.

What's more, associations of Catholic intellectuals and workers were beginning to recognize their new ability and obligation to affect events and were discussing ways in which they — predominantly lay people — could use the principles of the Christian myth to effect social change. Such Catholics are usually a small minority in any age. On the one hand, there is the deep-seated inertia among "ordinary Catholics" themselves; on the other hand, until very recently the official Church looked quite suspiciously on lay people acting as genuine adult Catholics.

In the latter half of the nineteenth century, there were only two (extraordinarily long-lived) popes: Pius IX, who governed longer than any pope in history, thirty-two years (1846–78), and Leo XIII, who governed for twenty-five years (1878–1903).

Pius IX was a preserver who believed a strong pope essential to preserving the fortress from dilution by adaptation to new ideas. As a result, the Church — a term now used almost exclusively to mean only the pope and his curia — adopted an unflinching stand against almost every intellectual, social, and political development that could be called "modern."

In the *Syllabus of Errors* (1864), Pius IX roundly condemned pantheism, naturalism, rationalism, Socialism, Communism, secret societies, Bible societies, liberal clerical groups, civil marriage, secular education for Catholics, religious indifferentism, and freedom of speech. "Catholic religion is the sole religion of the state, to the exclusion of all others" — so that "opinions and sentiments contrary to those of the Holy See may disappear."

Pius IX equivalently placed "the Church" in opposition to Liberalism in any form, no matter how remotely "liberal": even science, democracy, and tolerance. He was not merely saying only the Church was capable of discovering the truth, but he gave the impression the official Church determines the truth of natural law, rather than discovering that law in nature and scripture and articulating it. It was a new bloodless form of the Inquisition. Pius IX also summoned the first general council of bishops in three hundred years, and in 1870, against considerable opposition, political and theological, the first Vatican Council declared that, just as the Bible is without error, so is the pope — although the council fathers succeeded in limiting infallibility only to statements about faith and morals and only to occasions when the pope is speaking *ex cathedra*, that is, when he explicitly says he is speaking infallibly.

This gave rise to continued argument, as claims to absolute certitude always do. Strict adherents to the papacy fall victim to a kind of "creeping infallibility," so that every time the pope speaks on faith or morals, one's own personally reasoned conscience must obediently cave in: *Roma locuta, causa finita,* "Rome has spoken, the case is closed." What's more, infallibility even creeps out of Rome into what any cleric says, even when the individual believer is certain he or she knows more on a particular topic than the cleric does. Other more maverick types argue God gave us intelligence before God found need to give us the papacy, precious and essential as it is, or even the Commandments.

Conversion — The Church Rethinks Herself: 1900–1978

Leo XIII was the first "modern" pope, still traditional and conservative, but a man who thought in modern terms, who believed the Church can never allow herself to be isolated from the life of the culture in which she finds herself. Catholics could not shun all contact with "the world" out of some misplaced need to keep their faith "pure." In fact, in order to survive, the Church had to rise to her primary mission from Christ: to live in the world and evangelize it. And the world was Liberal, with all that means and in all its shadings. Leo was, in fact, ruthless against absolutist reactionaries who wanted to go back to the old ways. The Church can no longer dominate; she can only negotiate. With the development of radio, he began to speak frequently, directly to the people, rather than through letters or through the bishops.

If Leo XIII opposed Liberalism (laissez-faire Capitalism), it was insofar as Liberalism, with its resentment of government intrusion through labor laws, and so forth, was exploiting the working classes. Like St. Paul, he was an incurable letter writer, using his encyclicals as the *philosophes* had used their Encyclopedia: to educate the ordinary people.

In *Libertas* (1888), he affirmed what he saw good in political Liberalism, democracy, and freedom of conscience, thus draining at least some of the anti-intellectual poison of the *Syllabus of Errors*. *Immortale Dei* (1885) is, as Philip Hughes calls it, "the Magna Charta of the Catholic who believes in democracy," practical principles of how a Christian can be a loyal and contributing citizen in a secular state; it asserts that "no one should be forced to embrace the Catholic faith against his will."

His best-known letter is *Rerum Novarum* (1891), which means "Revolution." It dealt with the condition of the harrowing exploitation of the working classes, which Charles Dickens had captured so powerfully a few years earlier. In that letter, while insisting on the right to private property as essential to human freedom, Leo insisted also that private property is not an absolute right, but a right that has to be balanced by the more fundamental right of all human beings to food, shelter, and clothing — even if saving their lives means taking from the private property of others. Thus, the pope put the Church squarely on the side of social justice for workers, the poor, colonials, the disenfranchised, and squarely against the exploitations of monopoly capitalism. Right where Jesus had pointed us from the beginning.

Leo's successor, St. Pius X (1903–14) went back to the battlements. Pius X was a single-minded "thunderstorm," who refused to give an inch. Unlike most popes, he had been born poor, the son of the most detested form of government servant: a debt collector. Like so many absolutists, he saw everything as either yes or no, no maybes. The Church was all yes, and everything outside her was all no: democracy, psychology, science, the new biblical criticism, and freedom of thought. Everything outside the fortress Church was in conspiracy against it, and its name was "Modernism."

Anything unorthodox became automatically heterodox — heretical. Once again, the broad brush, the either/or mentality, wiped out any sense of a spectrum of shadings or degrees in the words "liberal" or "modern." Worse, it ignored the cautionary advice of the Rabbi Gamaliel: "If it is of God, nothing we can do will stop them." And worst, it ignored the words of Jesus himself: Judge a new movement not by its present appearance, but by its fruits.

But the enemies were not all outside the fortress. Pius X saw conspiracy within the walls as well: professors with crucial posts in universities, and more dangerously in seminaries, passing on the message of Christ perverted by these new, cynical sciences. Pius published the Index of Forbidden Books, which catalogued not just books of theology, philosophy, and science, but even novels and plays, which no priest could read without permission and which no lay person could read at all without, *ipso facto*, serious sin.

In his very first encyclical, Pius X declared, "We will take the greatest care to safeguard our clergy from being caught up in the snares of modern scientific thought." As a result, seminary professors were scrupulously and constantly scrutinized for any slightest sign of Modernist leanings, and many were dismissed from their posts and their writings added to the Index.

Benedict XV (1914–22) was elected pope two weeks after the beginning of the Great War. He refused to take sides, nor would he send emissaries to determine whether atrocities had been committed by either side, and thus was denounced by both. He made protests, especially to the Germans, regarding gassing, mistreatment of prisoners, and bombardments of civilian centers, but mostly through private communiqués, which could not be read by the general public as condemning either side. The Church gave away millions to the starving victims of the war, but Benedict continued his neutrality.

This was a totally new kind of war. On the one hand, the new sciences had made massive "progress" in the development of weapons, especially the airplane, which could bring war out of the fields, where wars had always been fought, into cities to destroy innocent civilians. For the first time in the history of Europe, the war was a wholly secular conflict, having nothing to do with religion. On the one side: Germany (Protestant), Austria (Catholic), Bulgaria (Orthodox), and Turkey (Muslim). On the other side: England (Protestant), France and Italy (Catholic), and Russia (Orthodox).

As later in World War II, individuals could find no way to put Christianity above their own nationalism. "Our" cause was the just one (i.e.,

God's), on both sides, and "our boys" were fighting for the "truth." In the end, the absolutist victors at Versailles imposed a treaty on the vanquished so humiliating and so economically devastating that it made a second war all but inevitable. Had there been anything genuinely and generously Christian in the aftermath of World War I, Adolf Hitler would have had no cause.

Pius XI (1922–39) was left to re-establish the Church among the shattered countries of Europe. Besides that, he established in the curia the Congregation for the Propagation of the Faith to revitalize the foreign missions, to assure that, with the close of the colonial era, native clergy would be able to shake off the patronizing of their former European masters. Modernism was now beginning to yield — or become merged with — Marxism, and Pius fought it single-mindedly and without distinctions of degree, not only in the newly arisen Soviet but in Spain, Mexico, and even in many Christian Democrat parties.

Pius XI was also a letter-writer. *Quadragesimo Anno*, "The Fortieth Year" (after *Rerum Novarum*), was a review of the whole question of capital and labor and their mutual responsibilities. But the most urgent problem bedeviling the world was the rise of totalitarianism in Italy and Germany. In 1931, *Non Abbiamo Bisogno* attacked the idea of the absolutist, omnicompetent State and made clear that no one could be both a true Catholic and a true Fascist. In 1937, *Mit Brennender Sorge* exposed "with shattering force" the Nazi mixture of fraud and cruelty and condemned the whole Nazi myth as immoral and anti-Christian. Five days later he fired off another lengthy letter on Communist tyranny in the Soviet Union.

The Church had shown a disastrous skill over the centuries in finetuning the words of doctrinal statements, but the modern popes, as we have seen, did not make even broad distinctions between Modernism and progress, liberalism and human freedom, communism and democracy. They did — by their silence — make a distinction in Fascism. Generalisimo Franco of Spain was admittedly a Fascist. But he defended the Church, as did most dictators of South America until very recently. It is difficult even for a loyal observer not to suspect that, once again, the Church's motives were at least at times opportunistic and self-serving.

At the urging of the papal nuncio to Germany, Eugenio Pacelli, Pius XI signed a Concordat with the Nazi government, only seven months after they had taken power, to protect Church interests in Germany and secure for Europe what it hoped would be an anti-communist bulwark. Most German bishops had no love for Hitler, but they feared communism, liberalism, and democracy even more.

In signing the concordat, however, Pius XI unilaterally emasculated any power the German Church had against Hitler — simply because the Church honored it and the Nazis didn't. In agreeing to withdraw "back into the sanctuary," he gave Hitler, in effect, legal basis to shut down the Catholic press, schools, societies, and clubs, including the far-reaching Catholic Youth, and requiring them to join the Hitler Youth — or risk their parents' jobs.

Hitler enacted a Pulpit Law to punish any clergyman who even remotely criticized the Nazi regime. Any priest was free to tell his people about the massacres of Jews and the undermining of the Church. But it would be his last public word. Nearly five hundred German and Austrian priests were interned in Dachau alone.

Hitler was a psychotic, who got worse the more he ingested power. But he was also an uncanny, intuitive, untutored strategist, with a "sense" of any enemy's weak spots and how far he could work them before he had to pay. He had good luck and, being a man utterly without conscience, had no restraints to prevent his using it. Hitler had vowed to rid his country of "the Jewish problem" and then "crush the Catholic Church like a toad."

Essentially, Nazism was no more and no less than the absolutist Catholicism Hitler had learned as a child in Austria — with every vestige of Christianity removed. Heinrich Himmler boasted that he had modeled the SS on the Society of Jesus. Again and again, Hitler spoke of himself in terms of a Messiah, appointed by "Providence" to bring salvation to the German people and the Aryan race. And the more he identified Germany with himself, the more every attack on either one became a blasphemy.

Pius XI died in 1939 as the inevitable war began, and Eugenio Pacelli was elected in a historic first ballot, unanimously. He took the name Pius XII (1939–58).

Although he wrote *Divino Afflante Spiritu*, liberating biblical scholars from the anti-Modernist chains of one hundred years, his tenure will probably be most remembered in history by his silence before the mechanical slaughter of six million Jews and ten million Slavs — because, to Hitler's satanic mind, they were "racial inferiors."

How could the pope be silent? The evidence is unarguable that Pius XII knew about the camps, the gassings, the inhuman treatment of prisoners, including thousands of his own priests. His defenders argue that a public protest would have changed nothing, that it would have posed an unbearable choice for German soldiers, who felt themselves both loyal Catholics and loyal Germans. There is something to indicate that was truly part of the pope's motivation; the papacy had rarely shown much trust for individual conscience.

But the most formidable argument for his silence seems rooted in the deeply embedded and longstanding papal fear of the infiltration of godless communism. Pius believed that, without a powerful wall in middle Europe, the Soviets would sweep in and gobble it up. And, on that score, he was tragically right.

But there is more. Pius XII was not just the pope; he was *this* pope. He was a painstakingly shaped and finely tuned Stradivarius. Throughout his seminary life, he was being groomed to be pope, like some Renaissance prince. Once ordained, he had little practice as an ordinary priest but spent his time fine-tuning diplomatic documents.

As a result, a scrupulously worded statement from such a man, which might have seemed to him an almost embarrassing outburst, was passed over by many who did not even realize he was angry. As we have seen so many times, subtlety and complexity don't "get through" to most people, even educated people. It is the oversimplifiers who motivate great movements — heresiarchs, Mohammed, Luther, Hitler, the Ayatollah. It was because Jesus' message, however simply and concretely stated, was complex that his disciples completely missed it most of the time. But to think of Eugenio Pacelli thundering through the Temple with a whip is to think the unthinkable. He was not Christ, only *this* man, trying to be Christian in the only way he knew.

It is wise to remember the truth put perhaps too crudely earlier: the great of history put on their socks one at a time.

Angelo Roncalli became Pope John XXIII (1958–63). He was in his late seventies, a compromise until a younger man could be "seasoned" for the job. But not since the four-year reign of Pius IV has such an explosion erupted in the Church! And it proved an explosion not unlike that first eruption on Pentecost.

Unlike Pius XII, John XXIII was an extrovert, talkative, loving to "touch flesh" with the people, and a man who truly enjoyed parish work. His two favorite words were *aggiornamento* ("updating") and *convivienza* ("gaiety"), and the old fortress was to get its quickest lesson in both in its history.

No sooner had John donned his white cassock than he was opening the fortress windows, reaching out to "our separated brethren," even opening communications with the communists! His two major encyclicals, in essence, negated the *Syllabus of Errors* and, for the first time in papal history, accepted total freedom of conscience. He suggested that we all might learn something even from communists, since practical consequences are more important than philosophical theory (at which time, half the popes buried in the Vatican turned over in their graves).

Within three months, he told his gaping curial cardinals he was calling a council. And not only that, he would invite all the separated brethren to take part — Orthodox, Protestants, Quakers — the whole Noah's Ark of Christians. Although the separated brethren came as observers, the between-meeting contacts, especially the *convivienza,* had an incalculable effect on Vatican Council II (1962–65). John did not live to see its conclusion, but he had unlocked the windows and taken the keys with him when he left.

Despite the foot-dragging of the curia, many of whom still viewed the Church and World as Augustine had, in pitched battle against one another, the council began. It was obvious John wanted a transfer of power from a monarchical papacy to the Church as a whole. The governing power was to be its congress of bishops, with the pope as a constitutional ruler. The Decree on the Church reads: "The body of the faithful cannot err in matters of belief. Thanks to a supernatural sense of the faith which characterizes the people as a whole, it manifests this unerring quality when, 'from the bishops down to the last member of the laity,' it shows universal agreement in matters of faith and morals."

John died before the second session, which was to unravel the whole question of Church lines of power. His successor, Paul VI (1963–78), inherited, as Paul Johnson puts it, "a democratic spirit but an autocratic machine." Many believed Paul feared schism, that traditionalists who fought for the fortress against Modernism (and now wanted to call the whole council off) would bolt the Church en masse if he continued John's optimistic acceptance of change, or that liberals would bolt if the changes weren't radical enough. Paul chose to walk the tightrope of compromise: The council would continue, but Paul withheld two topics from discussion: clerical celibacy and birth control.

In a very real sense, Paul hedged John's confident bet that a council of all the bishops in the world should be competent to settle such questions as ably as a single pope and his curia. When the issue of birth control inevitably arose in the council in discussions for the declaration on marriage and family, Pope Paul intervened and insisted there be no change.

John had set up an advisory committee that reported to Paul VI that the majority believed artificial birth control for unselfish reasons was not immoral. Against their findings, in July 1968, Paul published his encyclical *Humanae Vitae,* saying "each and every marriage act must remain open to the transmission of life." For both sides, the issue has become what Cardinal Suenens of Brussels predicted from the beginning: "a new 'Galileo affair.'"

The root of this problem is really a tangle of centuries-old problems. One is the flesh-despising Manichean spirit that dogged the Church from the beginning. Some think — wrongly, I believe — that another root of the official Church's inflexibility on genital questions is the same monarchical power we have seen so often in Church history or, worse, merely a group of old bachelors trying to keep people from enjoying themselves. Either opinion is mean-spirited.

Rather, I believe the official Church's single-minded stance on sexual questions is rooted in several other age-old truths. One, sex is very enjoyable. No denying that. Two, human sex is not the same as animal sex, not just a physical union but also a psychological union, which automatically makes human sexual questions complex. No denying that. Three, also lamentably proven throughout history, human beings don't really like wrestling with complex questions. No denying that. And, four, throughout history the official Church has shown herself too often like a loving but overprotective mother who doesn't want her babies (no matter what their age or education or experience) to get hurt.

As Bertrand Russell said, "Many people would rather die than think; most of them do." Thus, from the best of intentions, the Church steps in and does their thinking for them. But if all of us did learn how to think, and began to think seriously about the Church, then fearlessly stand up and offer what we've found to the Church, what an exciting Church that would be!

~ Questions for Discussion ~

1. Brainstorm the convictions about Christian belief about which everybody in the group is "absolutely certain." Once you've got a reasonably good list, sit back and look at them as devil's advocates — "heretics," if you will. Try to poke holes in them, find loopholes, uproot the areas where self-deception may have given the evidence more weight than the conclusion — the certitude — might be able to sustain. Chances are, when you finish, the conclusions will be still standing. But has temporarily doubting your certitudes led you to any richer insights?

2. Hindsight is the best sight of all, just as quarterbacking is easier on Monday. Read through the tragic — and yet somehow "right" — story of the Church in the twentieth century so far. Had you been pope, say, when Pius XII was, what would you have done? Now, play devil's advocate and listen to the dialogue that might have gone on inside the pope's head. Remember: one sock at a time.

Epilogue

Why Be Catholic?

THE INTRODUCTION SAID, "Animals can *know*, but only human beings can — to some degree — *understand*." We surely can understand God, Christianity, the Church, and ourselves, our souls, but only "to some degree."

Right there you have the whole point of the book, of the teaching and learning Church, perhaps the whole point of human life. When a Jew said "eternal life," he or she meant what we mean when we say "complete fulfillment as a human being." In John's gospel, Jesus tells us: "This is eternal life: to know you, the only true God, and Jesus Christ whom you have sent."

But as we have seen again and again, we "know" in three different but complementary ways. We know critically with the *left brain*, which analyzes the scriptures, spins out definitions, applies the answers of Jesus to the questions of today. We know intuitively with the *right brain*, which "senses" the fitness of an answer even before there is left-brain "proof," which has a "heart" that makes allowances, which meets God, beyond definitions, person-to-Person, in prayer. But we *understand* only with the soul, the whole "self," which fuses the inconclusive conclusions from both lobes into at least a tentative answer, a commitment, an act of faith.

Because we will always be imperfect, so will our answers about anything, from questions about the enormous carouse of the universe to questions about that same carouse reflected infinitesimally in a droplet of water. We will never have "the last word" on love, or suffering, or death. Our answers will always be imperfect, but endlessly improvable. Especially our answers about God, who deftly eludes all our definitions and symbols. As St. Paul says, "Who could ever know the mind of God?"

There is the paradox: Jesus says our whole purpose in life is to find the Mind of God, and yet St. Paul says we can never know it. That's not a contradiction, only a paradox, which just looks like a contradiction if you react to it too quickly. You can know; just don't expect to get God boxed into the perfect definition, and don't expect to get it all at once, as Adam and Eve did in the myth. Jesus' whole life was that lesson: He "emptied himself" in order to learn the only way a human can learn, step-by-step, and never certain. Whenever the Church, or any Christian, claims certitude, their claim says more about their arrogance than the content of the claim. Only God has certitude. Claiming certitude is, equivalently, blasphemy.

Certain words have come in for heavy bashing in these pages: "perfect," "absolute," "simplism," "single-minded." I hope I haven't made you "double-minded" (although doubtfulness is better than single-minded certitude; at least there's hope). "Double-minded" is just another way of saying you can't decide, that you're waiting for the "absolutely perfect" (and therefore unattainable) left-brain proof to overwhelm every shadow of doubt, or that you're waiting for the "absolutely perfect" rush of grace, a "sense" of the presence of God so powerful it will rape your assent. Don't wait for either. They're not coming.

I'm hoping you are *triple-minded*, like the Trinity in whose image you're made: coming to conclusions with the left and right brains and with the soul, the whole self, who says, "Yes."

Solid-but-admittedly-still-imperfect answers are not just not bad; they're the best you're ever going to get.

So, for anyone to look at the Church and either claim or demand she be perfect is asserting or requiring the impossible. For two thousand years, the old Chaste Whore has proven again and again, and yet again, it just can't be done. The surprising, no, the *miraculous*, thing about her is that she's up and moving, no matter what they throw at her and no matter how often she tries to cut her own throat.

One of the oldest metaphors for the Church is Peter's fishing boat. Good insights into the Church are packed into that metaphor: we're on a journey, with a map, lots of stormy weather, people falling overboard, pulling in survivors, mutinies among the crew, getting way off course, being attacked by pirates. And a boat needs a captain when everybody's losing their heads. But a ship also needs a crew, where each member knows his or her job, without the captain hovering over them every minute, not to mention his getting in their way.

The task of the Church, and each member, is to know the Triune God with our triune minds. We each have the left-brain task of thinking — gathering the data, sifting it, putting it into some kind of logical sequence — so we can draw a *personal* conclusion and put it out to be critiqued. Each of us.

The hierarchy — "the official Church" — must critique new doctrines offered from among the faithful, but always with the eye of Christ: giving the ideas enough time to see what kind of fruit they bear.

And the official Church — pope, bishops, theologians — has to consider all the new ideas and developments emerging outside the Church, to weigh them fairly and fearlessly, knowing genuine truth can never harm genuine religion; only ignoring or condemning genuine truth can harm it.

To repeat from the final chapter: The very *purpose* of the official Church is continuously to rethink the Person and message of Jesus Christ in the light of new and unexpected discoveries and to adapt and retranslate that message (1) without violating Jesus' original intentions and yet (2) honestly accommodating whatever is true in these new and unexpected discoveries and (3) explaining the final outcome in terms meaningful to the ever-evolving People of God.

The Church is neither a monarchy nor a democracy, neither an absolutist fortress commanded by an autocrat and manned by serfs nor a Christian self-improvement society like a therapy session with a few Jesus words thrown in. The people need the pope for trustworthy guidelines (a word less absolutist than "dogma" among adult Catholics). But the pope needs the people, and not just for spiritual and financial support, but for ideas — and for a forthright critique of his ideas.

There are two kinds of "authority." *Political* authority is conferred by election or inheritance or sheer brute force: the pope and bishops, the chairman of the board, the cop on the beat. *Moral* authority is not conferred but achieved, by study or experience or sheer bloody endurance: the theologian, the long-time teacher, people who have been married a long time.

They are different but *complementary* and genuine kinds of authority. The man or woman in the pew may not have a doctorate in theology, but then again the pope has never been married. In order for the Body of Christ to survive — much less avoid an endless un-civil cold war within itself — it needs the wisdom of all of its parts.

History is a homily, the story of the "tribe" we were born into. Hindsight is a way to know, to learn, whether it's watching the film of Saturday's game or discovering in the Church's history what the real relationship between Church and State or pope and people ought to be. And that history, as we've seen, however sketchily, has never been tranquil. Jesus said, "I haven't come to bring peace; I've come to bring disruption!" Not only is a difference of opinion unavoidable; it's *essential!*

New ideas are always painful, because acknowledging their truth means going back and rethinking it all again. But just as suffering is essential if a human being is to evolve into someone more fully human, so the effort of rethinking is essential if the Body of Christ is to evolve into the Kingdom Jesus envisioned. The Chaste Whore can never protect her purity from the "infection" of new ideas. Without syncretism — the angry battle over circumcision and the Jewish dietary laws, the wearisome task of rethinking the gospel with a Greek mind-set — we would never have had St. Paul, and quite possibly not a Christian Church at all.

One unhealthy rejection of syncretism concerned the foreign missions. When missionaries arrived in India, China, Japan, and the New World, they clung to the essentials of the gospel but tried to adapt the *understanding* of those essentials to customs of the places they were sent: dressing in rags with the poor and silks with the rich; teaching mathematics and geography to the learned, adapting Christian (European) symbols to the symbols meaningful to the common folk. In 1622, Gregory XV wrote:

> Do not bring any pressure to bear on the peoples to change their manners, customs and uses, unless they are evidently immoral. What could be more absurd than to transplant France, Spain, Italy, or some other European country to China? Do not introduce all that to them, but only the faith, which does not despise or destroy the manners and customs of any people.

Unfortunately, until quite recently, he was the only pope in history to feel that way. Everywhere missionaries went, churches began to flourish. Then, when some curial official came through for a relatively brief inspection (as in the film *The Mission*), all the syncretisms were ordered removed and the native services re-Europeanized. It was unthinkable. The only way a true Christian could pray was in Latin. Thus, the Christian Church in the Orient withered away.

Of course it's only wishful thinking, but "what if" China and Japan had been converted; after all, it had happened in a hostile, pagan Europe. The whole history of humankind would have changed, to say nothing of how enormously enriched all of us might have been if the gospel had been rethought in an Oriental mind-set. Pity.

We belong to a quite imperfect Church. History shows us that, undeniably. But if we are overly sensitive to the Church's failures, blindnesses, and blunders, it is very much the Church's own fault, because we are measuring her performance by her own thunderous claims. But if the life of Christ teaches us nothing, official Church and lay Christians alike, it teaches us that, for the Christian, *success is not the measure of accomplishment*. The focal symbol that embodies *all* that Christianity believes is the statue of a corpse, executed on a cross.

If you look to the Church for perfection, it's not there. If you look to the Church only for security, that's not there either. It was never intended to be. But if you look to the Church for challenge, for adventure, for evolution, oh, that's there, my friend — aplenty! We've come a long way, and we still have a lot further to go.

I doubt anyone can "leave the Church," any more than one can "leave" his or her family. When the Prodigal Son left home to seek his own way without his father's interference, he may have left the house, but he didn't stop being a member of the family. He may have been a remiss and ungrateful son; he may never have written or come for a visit on the holidays; but he never stopped being a son of that father, or part of that unique family. He could no more have foresworn his family than he could have rejected his DNA. As they said about James Joyce, "You could take the boy out of the Church, but you couldn't take the Church out of the boy." They may be "non-practicing Catholics," but they're still Catholics.

People say they've "left the Church" when they stop going to Mass. The real reason we go to Mass is an act of gratitude to the One who invited us into . . . everything. It's also a way to remind ourselves we were not born to be nobodies; we were born to make a difference; we are Peers of the Realm: *noblesse oblige.* And when we're not feeling overly "somebody," all those other people remind us that we're not in this alone.

If you give it an honest chance, the Mass can be a reminder that our innermost selves, our souls, are entities "outside it all." If we can just let loose the defenses and pretenses, the messed-up priorities, we can begin to understand our true *selves,* alien beings who live in the "Great Outside It All." *Right now!*

The historian Paul Johnson writes: "Man is imperfect with God. Without God, what is he?" And he quotes the thirteenth-century scientist Roger Bacon: "Certainly man is of kin to beasts by his body. And, if he be not kin to God by his spirit, he is a base and ignoble creature."

If you've come this far, you don't know all there is to know about God, or Christianity, or the Catholic Church. Or yourself. Neither, thank God, do I. Learning more will keep us both alive, evolving. But as a result of this book, we both now know more than we did.

And that's just fine.

Finally, brothers and sisters, fill your minds with everything that is true, everything that is noble, everything good and pure, everything we love and honor, and everything that can be called virtuous or worthy of praise. . . . Then the God of peace will be with you.
— Philippians 4:8–9

OF RELATED INTEREST

Msgr. Lorenzo Albacete

GOD AT THE RITZ

A Priest-Physicist Talks About Science, Sex, Politics, and Religion

"Lorenzo Albacete is one of a kind, and so is God at the Ritz. The book like
the monsignor crackles with humor, warmth, and intellectual excitement.
Reading it is like having a stay-up-all-night, jump-out-of-your-chair,
have-another-double-espresso marathon conversation with one of the world's most
swashbuckling talkers. Conversation, heck - this is a Papal bull session!"
—-HENDRIK HERZBERG, *The New Yorker Magazine*

A former NASA physicist and friend of Pope John Paul II offers a thoughtful,
timely, and often whimsical look at why religion still matters. Albacete writes a
column on religion for *The New York Times Sunday Magazine.*

0-8245-1951-5 $19.95 hardcover

Luigi Giussani

THE RISK OF EDUCATION

Discovering Our Ultimate Destiny

Catholic Leader Prescribes Remedy for What Is Ailing Our Educational System

The fundamental idea in the education of the young is the fact that it is through
the younger generations that society successively rebuilds itself; therefore, the
primary concern of society is to teach the young. What does education consist of,
and how does it take place? Giussani embraces our core as human beings, and
presents a fundamental guide for teachers and educators who are striving to
understand the important role they have in educating the youth of today. Written
from a Christian viewpoint, the book faithfully examines the rationale for education:
how to educate ourselves, what education is, and how real education comes about.

0-8245-1899-3 $16.95 paperback

OF RELATED INTEREST

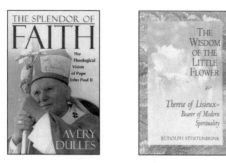

Avery Cardinal Dulles
THE SPLENDOR OF FAITH
The Theological Vision of Pope John Paul II

"Dulles' synthesis is a splendid achievement and is warmly recommended
to all who would understand the mind of the premier witness to the
gospel of Jesus Christ in our time."—FIRST THINGS

A philosopher and theologian, as well as priest, bishop, and finally pope, John Paul
II has written extensively on a wide variety of subjects. With his considerable theological expertise and acumen, Avery Dulles has undertaken the demanding task of
synthesizing The Pope's theological insights on the complete range of topics from the
Trinity and Christology to the economic and social order. In clear and lucid prose,
Dulles enters into the thought of John Paul II and reveals the main outlines of his
theological vision—a truly comprehensive vision that deserves to be seen as a whole.

0-8245-1792-X $21.95 paperback

Rudolf Stertenbrink
THE WISDOM OF THE LITTLE FLOWER
Therese of Lisieux—Bearer of Modern Spirituality
Beloved Saint Enters the Mainstream!

Millions of people around the world, including The Pope, are devoted aficionados
of a modest young nun who died early last century. What is the secret of
Therese of Lisieux who is one of only three women who were awarded
the exclusive title of "Doctor of the Church?"

St. Therese of Lisieux believed that what matters most in life is not high theology, but
hope against all adversity. In this engrossing book, Stertenbrink unearths the more
thoughtful side of this simple nun. In doing so, he quotes from Dostoyevsky,
Kierkegaard, Cardinal Newman and Edith Stein, among others. The result is a direct
encounter with Therese. The book is comprised of short essays that can be read one
at a time—before bed or on the train—or straight through for a compelling narrative.

0-8245-1983-3 $17.95 paperback

OF RELATED INTEREST

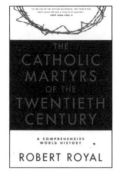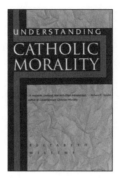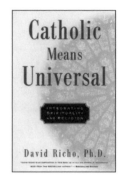

Robert Royal

CATHOLIC MARTYRS OF THE TWENTIETH CENTURY
A Comprehensive World History

Robert Royal presents the first comprehensive history of the twentieth-century
martyrs. This volume traces specific situations all over the world, accounts
how martyrdoms occurred, studies the political systems, and
offers a rich collection of individual biographies.

0-8245-1846-2 $39.95 hardcover

Elizabeth L. Willems

UNDERSTANDING CATHOLIC MORALITY

This concise and well-written text focuses on development, not simply
the acquisition of learning about Catholic morality. An ideal addition
for personal or classroom study.

0-8245-1725-3 $19.95 paperback

David Richo

CATHOLIC MEANS UNIVERSAL
Integrating Spirituality and Religion

David Richo teaches that the spiritual traditions of Roman Catholicism point
to a body of truths common to all. His message is for all seekers, in and
out of the Church, looking for a deeper experience of self and God.

0-8245-1837-3 $16.95 paperback

OF RELATED INTEREST

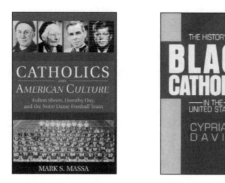

Mark Massa, S.J.

CATHOLICS AND AMERICAN CULTURE
Fulton Sheen, Dorothy Day, and the Notre Dame Football Team

While in the early years of the century Catholics in America were for the most part distrusted outsiders with respect to the dominant culture, by the 1960s the mainstream of American Catholicism was in many ways "the culture's loudest and most uncritical cheerleader." Mark Massa explores the rich irony in this postwar transition, beginning with the heresy case of Leonard Feeney, examining key figures such as Fulton Sheen, Thomas Merton, and John F. Kennedy, and concluding with a look at the University of Notre Dame and the transformed status of American Catholic higher education.

0-8245-1955-8 $24.95 paperback

Cyprian Davis

THE HISTORY OF BLACK CATHOLICS IN THE UNITES STATES

"This book makes an extremely valuable contribution to our understanding of African-American religious life by presenting the first full-length treatment of the Black Catholic experience. This study should be read by all interested in the history and culture of Black Americans."—ALBERT RABOTEAU, Princeton University

This book is the story of a people who maintained their identity as African Americans and their pride in their Catholic identity. Written from the vantage point of black Catholics themselves, is the story of militant action combined with sincere piety and an unswerving devotion to a church that they insisted on calling their own.

0-8245-1495-5 $24.95 paperback

OF RELATED INTEREST

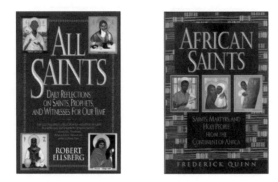

Robert Ellsberg

ALL SAINTS

Daily Reflections on Saints, Prophets, and Witnesses for Our Time

WINNER OF THE 1998 CHRISTOPHER AWARD

"A Wonderfully broad, knowing, and narratively compelling look at
human goodness as it has been tested by life—this book will give us the very best
kind of moral and spiritual education."—ROBERT COLES

0-8245-1679-6, $24.95 paperback

Frederick Quinn

AFRICAN SAINTS

Saints, Martyrs, and Holy People From the Continent of Africa

"The official calendar of the saints has long been weighted toward the West. But in
this era of the 'world church' it is more important than ever to draw on the inspiration and challenge of holy people from other parts of the world. This important
book reminds us of the vital contributions of the African church, greatly expanding
that 'cloud of witnesses' who inspire and challenge us on our path to holiness."
—ROBERT ELLSBERG, Editor-in-Chief of Orbis Books, and author of *All Saints*

0-8245-1971-X $22.95 paperback

Please support your local bookstore, or call 1-800-707-0670.

For a free catalog, please write us at:
The Crossroad Publishing Co.
481 Eighth Avenue, Suite 1550, New York, NY 10001
www.crossroadpublishing.com

All prices subject to change.

WHY BE CATHOLIC?

OTHER BOOKS BY
WILLIAM J. O'MALLEY, S.J.

Meeting the Living God

The Fifth Week

A Book about Praying

The Roots of Unbelief

Scripture and Myth

How the Gospels Work

The Voice of Blood

Phoenix

Love and Justice

Why Not?

Daily Prayers for Busy People

Converting the Baptized

Building Your Own Conscience
(Batteries Not Included)

Becoming a Catechist
(Ways to Outfox Teenage Skepticism)

Yielding: Prayer for Those in Need of Hope